# PRAISE FOR *REVOLUTIONIZE ASSESSMENT*

I want to put this book and these ideas in the hands of every teacher and school leader in America. We need to support learning, not merely measure it.

Sharon Robinson
Executive Director, American Association of Colleges of
Teacher Education and of the Learning First Alliance
Washington

This book is a plea from the heart, from 50+ years of experience, from someone who has immersed himself in the research, the classroom, the professional learning communities and the publication business—and Stiggins sees it all too clearly. It is time to fix the assessment problem. There is more packed into this little treatise than in encyclopedias on this topic. There is passion, wisdom, and a critical message—it is not too late, but move soon. A clear blueprint is outlined as to the path to follow.

John Hattie
Professor of Educational Research
University of Melbourne
Australia

In this concise, compelling, and readable book, Rick Stiggins explains clearly the extraordinary damage that has been done to America's youth by the belief that standardized testing is the only, or even the best, way to find out what students have learned. He also shows how more appropriate assessment, in which learners play a leading role, has the power to transform American education. Anyone interested in what is wrong with education in America today—and what we can do about it—should read this book.

Dylan Wiliam
Emeritus Professor of Educational Assessment
Institute of Education, University of London

Noted authority Rick Stiggins offers an important "wake up call" as he documents how our nation has lost its way on the assessment road, and offers we can reclaim the promise of assessments that truly support meaningful learning.

Jay McTighe
Co-author of the *Understanding by Design®* series
Author of *Core Learning: Assessing What Matters Most*

Every once and awhile a book appears that is so honest, so sensible, and so impassioned that it must not be ignored. This is such a book, and it will make many education policy makers and assessment experts wince. Stiggins decries the damage done by poorly designed tests and thoughtless assessment practice. Thankfully, he doesn't stop with an indictment. Drawing on a half century of experience, Stiggins offers practical advice on how sound assessment practice can benefit all students.

Dan Duke
Professor of Educational Leadership
University of Virginia

In this powerful book Rick Stiggins—through story, research, and practical ideas—clearly offers ways to transform what seem to be overwhelming roadblocks to learning by involving students and using high quality classroom assessment. This book is an important tool for all leaders as they pursue success for all learners.

Anne Davies
Connect2Learning
British Columbia, Canada

# REVOLUTIONIZE
# ASSESSMENT

*For Doris Sperling, who helped me see the
student inside every assessment, for Professor Henry Morlock,
SUNY Plattsburgh, and in memory of Robert Ebel,
Michigan State University, both of whom helped me learn to
speak for those students*

# REVOLUTIONIZE
# ASSESSMENT

Empower
Students,
Inspire
Learning

# RICK STIGGINS

Foreword by Michael Fullan

CORWIN
A SAGE Company

**CORWIN**
A SAGE Company

FOR INFORMATION:

Corwin

A SAGE Company

2455 Teller Road

Thousand Oaks, California 91320

(800) 233-9936

www.corwin.com

SAGE Publications Ltd.

1 Oliver's Yard

55 City Road

London EC1Y 1SP

United Kingdom

SAGE Publications India Pvt. Ltd.

B 1/I 1 Mohan Cooperative Industrial Area

Mathura Road, New Delhi 110 044

India

SAGE Publications Asia-Pacific Pte. Ltd.

3 Church Street

#10-04 Samsung Hub

Singapore 049483

Printed in the United States of America.

A catalog record of this book is available from the Library of Congress.

ISBN: 978-1-4833-5935-9

This book is printed on acid-free paper.

Executive Editor:   Arnis Burvikovs

Associate Editor:   Desirée A. Bartlett

Editorial Assistant:   Ariel Price

Production Editor:   Cassandra Margaret Seibel

Copy Editor:   Kate Macomber Stern

Typesetter:   C&M Digitals (P) Ltd.

Proofreader:   Jen Grubba

Indexer:   Terri Corry

Cover Designer:   Karine Hovsepian

Certified Sourcing
www.sfiprogram.org
SFI-00453

SFI label applies to text stock

14 15 16 17 18 10 9 8 7 6 5 4 3 2 1

# Contents

# Foreword

Rick Stiggins has spent his professional life working with students, teachers, school leaders—and assessments—and this book recounts the evolution of his thinking about how best to use assessment to improve education. Stiggins understands the uses and misuses of assessments, but he sees there has been much more of the latter—especially with the increasing use of high-stakes annual standardized tests. He explains the problems and their solutions in such a comprehensive and compelling way, we may finally get some action on the phenomenon of assessment.

Drawing on detailed research evidence and his own close work with practitioners and researchers, Stiggins leaves no stone unturned. He shows how and why assessment, which started off as a great potential source of improvement for what ails schools, has become the single biggest albatross in the reform package. The first four chapters not only document the problem of current assessment, but also show how and why we have become mired in a vicious circle of wasted effort and resources in the billions of dollars. No one can read these chapters without increasing dismay.

Chapter 4 brings this bad pre-history into focus, by addressing head on the issue of why annual testing has not improved schools. The culprit is the naïve assumption of policy makers about the role of testing combined with a massive lack of assessment expertise at all levels. The bottom line is that there is almost no focus in the system on examining the impact of testing on day-to-day teaching or on learning and student success. Having revealed the "assessment emperor" as having no clothes, Stiggins spends the remaining three chapters mapping out a fundamentally different role for assessment.

We are then treated to a wonderfully clear and inspiring chapter on a new assessment vision for schools, including a powerful, insightful section on "the emotional dynamics of being evaluated." With this vision as a foundation Stiggins turns to strategy, starting with the roles of school and district leaders. He formulates three "local priorities"—very clear, specific, and doable.

In the final chapter Stiggins offers specific suggestions about how to implement useful assessments that contribute to student learning, this time speaking specifically to the measurement community and testing industry. *Revolutionize Assessment* is both a deeply personal and professional book, and it weaves these two dimensions together beautifully. The message is clear, it is essential, and it is both a cry of frustration and a solution delivered on a platter. It is time to re-position assessment. Rick Stiggins has given us the ideas and tools to do so—a great legacy.

Michael Fullan
Professor Emeritus
OISE/University of Toronto

# Acknowledgments

When I began my exploration of the world of classroom assessment, I could find no professional network in the United States to guide me. Luckily, I was able to find a partnership with colleagues north of the border in Canada, so first and foremost, I thank them for taking me in and allowing me to learn. The foundation of my understanding of the realm of classroom assessment and many of the ideas and strategies I have taught to teachers comes from kindred spirits in Canada, including but certainly not limited to Anne Davies, Lorna Earl, and Ken O'Connor.

During my early years of classroom assessment work, it became clear that some of the best research and development in this realm was being conducted outside of the United States, so I became part of an international team to continue my learning. Those from whom I learned the most included Linda Allal of Switzerland, Ruth Sutton and Dylan Wiliam from the United Kingdom, Royce Sadler and John Hattie from Australia, and Terry Crooks of New Zealand.

My journey to understanding classroom assessment and its role in promoting student well-being has spanned decades. This book represents my attempt to inform those who follow us into this realm of study what we have learned and what remains to be learned. My thinking and my beliefs during this journey have been guided most of all by my teammates at the Assessment Training Institute: Jan Chappuis, Steve Chappuis, Judy Arter, and Sharon Lippert, as well as associate Carol Commodore. Special thanks also to my beloved wife, Nancy Bridgeford, for taking the leap of faith with me to create ATI.

Over the past two years, as I drafted, revised, and worried over the preparation of this book, I was guided by a professional network whose patience I greatly appreciate. At times my ideas were strong but my text was weak, and other times the ideas themselves were in need of guided revision. That guidance has been provided by Sharon Robinson, Dan Duke, Dick Streedain, Sarah Gandolfo, Jim Popham, Stephen Uebbing, Cyndie Schmeiser, Kati Haycock, and Vicki Spandel. Special thanks to Kate Macomber Stern, whose writing skills can transform.

Thanks to all of you for helping me understand.

# About the Author

**Rick Stiggins** is the founder and retired president of the Assessment Training Institute (ATI), Portland, Oregon, a professional development company providing teachers and school leaders with the assessment literacy needed to face the assessment challenges in American education today. He is a native of Canandaigua, NY, and a graduate of the State University of New York at Plattsburgh, where he majored in psychology. He holds a master's degree in industrial psychology from Springfield (MA) College and a Ph.D. in educational measurement from Michigan State University.

Prior to launching ATI in 1992, Rick served on the College of Education faculties of Michigan State University, the University of Minnesota, and Lewis and Clark College, Portland, OR. He was director of test development at ACT in Iowa City, directed performance assessment and classroom assessment research and development programs at the Northwest Regional Educational Laboratory in Portland, OR, and has been a visiting scholar at Stanford University and the University of Southern Maine.

After conducting a decade of in-school research on the state and status of classroom assessment in United States' schools, Rick authored an introductory textbook for teachers on classroom assessment, *An Introduction to Classroom Assessment FOR Student Learning*, now in its sixth edition. He has authored numerous other print, video, and online pre- and in-service training programs used by teachers and school leaders to improve assessment practice. Rick and his ATI team have helped hundreds of thousands of teachers and school leaders from across the country and around the world learn to gather accurate evidence of student achievement and to use the assessment process to support, rather than merely to grade, student learning. The most important aspect of this work is ATI's development of the idea of "assessment FOR learning," a classroom practice that uses ongoing self-assessment to sustain student growth and confidence.

*People who live in difficult circumstances need to know that happy endings are possible.*

Supreme Court Justice
Sonia Sotomayor,
*My Beloved World*

# 1

# A Hidden Crisis in American Education

*Do not go where the path may lead, go instead where there is no path and leave a trail.*

Ralph Waldo Emerson

While annual accountability standardized testing has raised awareness of some of the problems schools face, it has done little to help us solve those problems. In that sense, it has let us down as a "school improvement" strategy. This does not mean we should stop annual testing. Schools are public institutions and the public is entitled to evidence of student achievement. It merely means we must stop believing that this particular application of assessment can promote much by way of greater student learning. There are specific and completely understandable reasons for this and I will detail them shortly. As you will see, their instructional inadequacy arises from the nature of the tests themselves and the environment in which they are used.

At the same time, however, we must understand that, under the right conditions, there are other assessment practices which can have a profoundly positive impact on student learning success. Unfortunately, those conditions have rarely been satisfied in

American schools. That is why the time has come for us to face up to and address the dire state of our local, state, and national assessment affairs. We have reached a stage in the development of the American educational system when we need to be able to count on assessment to live up to its full potential as a dynamic tool for teaching and learning. To date, that confidence has not been earned.

Research and development efforts conducted over the past two decades around the world have provided us with ideas, tools, and strategies needed to succeed at this. This book maps a pathway to this new and more powerful vision of excellence in assessment. Now we need the will and dedication to complete the journey, both of which have been missing to date.

## A TIME FOR REVOLUTION

This book represents the culmination of fifty years of my escalating discomfort with our national, state, and local assessment policies and practices. It's time to issue a wakeup call to all who care about school quality, including parents, educators, federal, state, and local policy makers, and community leaders. Our testing practices are in crisis. They are currently doing as much harm as good for student learning.

My concerns about the state or our assessment affairs arose during my graduate studies at Michigan State University in the 1970s. That was when I first became aware of how ill-prepared local teachers and school leaders were to deal in productive ways with the assessment challenges they faced. For example, I realized leaders had no training in and little sense of how to interpret or use annual standardized test scores. Teachers were provided with no preparation in how to create quality classroom assessments or how to communicate with others about the achievement of their students using either test scores or report card grades.

My worries continued to grow through the early years of my career as I saw local educators spending immense resources on annual standardized testing, only to file the results away unused because they could find no way to link them to instructional improvement. The test results were neither instructionally helpful to them nor relevant to classroom practice. This was when I identified the crux of our assessment problem: in the field of education, there are those who test and those who teach, and never the twain shall meet! These professionals lived (and continue to live) in separate, disconnected professional worlds.

My fears have escalated over the past decade, as I have watched federal and state political leaders naively turn to annual accountability testing as their means of intimidating educators into changing their schools. Their well-intentioned but misdirected policies reveal a deep misunderstanding of the testing process and how it fits (or can fit) into effective schooling. Often, their policies are harming as many teachers and students as they help. They are driving many of our best teachers and local school leaders from the profession, and the consequences for our students are dire.

This need not be so, as our educational assessments really could drive immense school improvement. They can only do so, however, if those involved in their use understand how to shape those tests and how to interpret and apply results effectively. Currently, and with all due respect, typically, neither our highest level policy makers nor our in-school practitioners have developed that understanding.

Traditional testing practices in the United States are based on instructional and motivational principles that cause many students to give up in hopelessness and accept failure rather than driving them enthusiastically toward academic success. This is one of the reasons why national achievement, as measured by our National Assessment of Educational Progress (NAEP), has flat-lined for decades, our place as a nation in international comparisons of achievement remains doggedly and disconcertingly in the middle of the pack, dropout rates remain unacceptably high, the achievement gaps that have troubled us for so long persist, and some of our most able students fail to reach their full academic potential. Our testing policies and practices, which should be helping us address these realities, are in fact one of their causes.

We can turn things around, though, and we must. A determined international network of assessment specialists, university faculty, classroom teachers, school administrators, researchers, and policy leaders has spent the past twenty years confronting this crisis. We have uncovered new ways to use assessment to transform our schools into genuine places of learning—places where students come to believe in themselves as successful learners. Collectively, we believe this is important because assessment—*the process of measuring student achievement and using results to inform instructional decisions*—may offer more promise for promoting learner success than any other instructional practice or school improvement innovation we have at our disposal. But we have to use it wisely. Promise and potential will never become reality until local communities demand that their schools *use assessment differently* from the way it has been used in the past.

Our chronic assessment problems arise from the same source: a widespread lack of training in, and therefore understanding of, sound assessment practice among teachers, principals, district leaders, and state education leaders. Most readily acknowledge their lack of assessment literacy and decry their lack of opportunity to become assessment literate. Unfortunately, the policy makers who could make available the resources needed to permit that training (a) remain largely unaware of this gap in the collective professional competence of school personnel, and (b) typically have little background in sound assessment practice themselves. As a result, they create unsound assessment policies that are implemented by unqualified faculty and staff to the detriment of our students.

We must either provide our professional educators and education policy makers with the understanding they need to do their jobs—especially in the assessment realm—or we must stop claiming to care about the achievement gap and school improvement.

A revolution in assessment practices may be needed to prevent a revolution of a different sort among the ranks of practicing educators. Teachers are striking over this issue. In 2013, the American Federation of Teachers launched a nation-wide political and media campaign to stem over-emphasis on standardized test scores. Parents are withdrawing their children from testing programs. Local school leaders are throwing up their arms in frustration. Consider the following excerpts from a letter to the parents from members of the New York Principals.[1] It lists sixteen issues to be addressed in the state tests and was turned over to the New York Department of Education bearing 3700 signatures (endorsements) of New York educators. I have selected just a few of their concerns for inclusion here to illustrate the nature and depth of the authors' apprehension:

> This year, many of your children experienced the first administration of the newly revised New York State Assessments.

You may have heard that teachers, administrators, and parents are questioning the validity of these tests. As dedicated administrators, we have carefully observed the testing process and have learned a great deal about these tests and their impact. We care deeply about your children and their learning and want to share with you what we know—and what we do not know—about these new state assessments.

**Here is what we know:**

- **NYS Testing Has Increased Dramatically:** We know that our students are spending more time taking State tests than ever before. Since 2010, the amount of time spent on average taking the 3–8 ELA [English, Language Arts] and Math tests has increased by a whopping 128%! The increase has been particularly hard on our younger students, with third graders seeing an increase of 163%!

- **The Tests Were Too Long:** We know that many students were unable to complete the tests in the allotted time. Not only were the tests lengthy and challenging, but embedded field test questions extended the length of the tests and caused mental exhaustion, often before students reached the questions that counted toward their scores.

- **Ambiguous Questions Appeared Throughout the Exams:** We know that many teachers and principals could not agree on the correct answers to ambiguous questions in both ELA and Math. . . .

- **Children Have Reacted Viscerally to the Tests:** We know that many children cried during or after testing. . . .

**Here is what we don't know:**

- **How to Use These Tests to Improve Student Skills or Understanding:** Tests should serve as a tool for assessing student skills and understanding. Since we are not informed of the make-up of the tests, we do not know, with any specificity, the content or skills for which children require additional support.

- **The Underlying Cause of Low Scores:** We do not know if children's low test scores are actually due to the lack of skills in that area or simply a case of not finishing the test—a problem that plagued many students. . . . (New York Principals, 2013, pp. 2 and 5)

Productive revolutions have been unfolding around us in many fields of professional practice. Discoveries in medicine have extended life for millions and revolutionized the ways in which medicine is practiced. Discoveries in science and technology have expanded our known universe and revolutionized our daily digital lives. Now, thanks to discoveries in the field of educational assessment, we are poised to revolutionize student learning—and *that* is a revolution which promises to impact every other aspect of our lives, from medicine to technology and beyond. This revolution, like many, needs to begin small: right in the classroom.

John Hattie and his colleagues at the University of Auckland, New Zealand, reported significant gains in student achievement through the careful management of classroom assessment as an instructional intervention (Hattie & Timperley, 2007). Dylan Wiliam and Paul Black (1998) of Kings College, London, have synthesized research on this topic and concluded that we could quite literally double the rate of student learning simply by using day-to-day classroom assessments in more thoughtful, purposeful ways. Others exploring new assessment applications in Norway, Finland, Canada, Scotland, Wales, France, and Switzerland, among other nations, are adding to our understanding of how to use classroom assessment to revitalize student learning success.

For decades, as a society, we have clung to the notion of assessment as a tool for holding students and schools accountable. This is not wholly inappropriate, but it is way too narrow. While it is appropriate to expect our schools to present evidence of student learning, true accountability takes more than shrill demands. It requires implementation of quality assessments by people who understand both the potential and the limitations of testing. Our continuous cry for higher annual test scores—as if these were the only or even the best measure of school effectiveness—has so deafened our social and political discourse that we fail to hear whispers of exciting new assessment ideas now circling the educational globe.

We must begin by asking what it is we expect from our schools, recognizing the mission we have assigned to schools has changed dramatically in recent years. We now demand that schools narrow achievement gaps and demonstrate increasingly higher levels of achievement among students at all levels. In order for assessment to be effective, or even useful, we must ensure that our assessment practices align with this new mission. If they do not, the achievement gap that troubles us so deeply will not narrow, and our students will not attain the lifelong learner competence in reading, writing, or math problem solving that we need for our society to thrive.

It seems logical to most of us that assessment is a key to improving student performance, but the question is, what do we do with that insight? This has been our answer: If students are not doing as well as expected, we test them more—and if that doesn't work, we make our standards and expectations more stringent and demand even more testing. The problem is, the answer to improved student performance rests with instruction; however, to be maximally effective that instruction must work in continuous, close harmony with good assessment. Optimally, instruction and assessment need to occur almost simultaneously, whereas at present, only instruction is continuous with assessment attached somewhere at the end of it. They are all too often working at cross purposes. The long-standing barriers that have separated testing from teaching have rendered assessment essentially powerless to improve schools—and these barriers must come down. Recent research on the practice of assessment and psychology of learning has revealed important insights about how to make this happen.

Along with colleagues at the Assessment Training Institute in Portland, Oregon, I have spent thirty years transforming the results of that research into professional development programs specifically designed to help teachers and local school leaders become competent assessors. Participants in this training learned to use classroom assessment to increase student confidence, engage students in managing their own learning, and foster higher levels of achievement than many of their students had ever dreamed possible.

In the chapters that follow, we discuss *why we assess*, *what we assess*, and *how we assess* in order to establish what it means to do it right and why it is so crucial to student well-being that we do so.

We will use stories from the classroom to contrast our current outdated vision of excellence in assessment with a new assessment vision that can turn schools around. The old vision merely used assessment to grade student learning—to hold students accountable for learning—while the new vision encourages students to play an active role, actually making important instructional decisions as they learn. This difference between assessment OF learning and assessment FOR learning represents a dramatic breakthrough.

Research on the psychology of learning offers a compass and roadmap to guide us. It involves three critical elements—we will address each of these as my presentation unfolds:

- Using assessment to generate new learning, not just grade it;
- Relying on learning success rather than intimidation and anxiety to motivate students;
- Increasing the positive impact of instruction for all by increasing the quality of our day-to-day classroom assessments.

## ONE MESSAGE TO MANY AUDIENCES

Several audiences have a stake in the quality of schools and student well-being: family members concerned about their children, local community leaders, professional educators, education policy makers, and testing professionals. These stakeholders bring different concerns, backgrounds, and interests to the topic of school quality. But, unless we agree on a productive vision of excellence in assessment, productive local improvement will remain out of reach.

From time to time, it will be necessary for me to speak directly to specific stakeholders, but I encourage others to eavesdrop. The more each of us understands the role(s) of others, the easier it will become to understand, value, and embrace a new far more promising vision of educational assessment. There can be no more hidden messages or agendas. Our only concern must be the learning success of our students and, by implication, the professional success of their teachers.

If you hear passion in my voice, it is because I was a struggling learner (I will tell you that story in Chapter 3). As a result, I am driven by a deep concern for the well-being of all students, but especially those who become trapped by their own failure and their inability to find the way out. Branding them with unflattering labels, as our assessment systems often do, is unwise, unfair, counterproductive, and harmful. Anyone who does harm to vulnerable second, third, or any "graders" is going to have to live with the consequences.

But my concern also extends to our most able learners. They too can become victims of assessment systems which encourage the pursuit of good grades rather than true understanding of important ideas and mastery of skills. Those who fall prey to this motivational trap will not reach their learning potential, and the rest of us will never benefit from the leadership, wisdom, or discoveries they might have offered. This need not happen. We have choices. We know better and we can do better—very much better—and that is precisely what this book is about.

## ENDNOTE

1. The following principals contributed to this letter: Carol Burris, EdD, Principal, South Side High School; Peter DeWitt, EdD, Principal, Poestenkill Elementary; Tim Farley, Principal, Ichabod Crane Middle School; Sean C. Feeney, PhD, Principal, The Wheatley School; Sharon Fougner, Principal, E.M. Baker Elementary; Andrew Greene, Principal, Candlewood Middle School; Elizabeth Phillips, Principal, P.S. 321; Katie Zahedi, PhD, Principal, Linden Avenue Middle School

# 2

# To Begin With, We Must Understand This Realm of Educational Assessment

*. . . it is not unreasonable to believe that the educational significance of locally produced classroom tests may far outweigh that of the occasional standardized test. . . .*

Robert L. Ebel

Because of decades of increasing use of layer upon layer of annual standardized testing, that relatively small corner of the realm of assessment has become a light so brilliant in our eyes that we have difficulty seeing past it. But when we switch off that light, what becomes visible is a wide range of ways to evaluate student learning and an array of strategies for using the assessment process and its results that truly can benefit student learning. They play out, not once a year, but day to day in our classrooms. If we are to build a world class educational system in the United States, it is crucial that we develop an all-inclusive assessment concept, one where annual testing is only a tiny part. I outline that broader concept below by describing why, what, and how we assess student achievement in schools and how we communicate results. This primer will form the backdrop for the vision of excellence in assessment I describe throughout the rest of the book.

As we go, keep in mind that assessment is the process of gathering evidence of student learning for the purpose of informing instructional decisions. Good evidence leads to good decisions and greater student learning; poor quality evidence feeds into counterproductive decisions that inhibit learning.

## WHY WE ASSESS

The list of reasons for evaluating student learning is surprisingly long. The array of assessment users and uses begins in the classroom and fans outward from there.

We all know that teachers gather achievement evidence during a grading period in order to make decisions about what grade to give a student on a report card. In other words, one reason teachers assess is to verify or certify student learning. But that's far from the only reason why educators assess student achievement.

Teachers also gather information in the moment to decide how far an individual student has progressed in her or his learning and what should come next or to find out whether their instructional strategy is working. Sometimes teachers' decisions center on how to assist an individual student and other times an entire class. The practice of classroom assessment is the art of knowing what information is needed for each decision, how to gather it, and how to use it effectively.

Finally, teachers use the promise of upcoming assessment to motivate students to invest the time and energy needed to learn. In this sense, assessment helps students understand that they will be held accountable for their learning success or failure.

The list of decision makers/assessment users doesn't stop with teachers. School building principals and school district instructional leaders must rely on assessment results to determine the quality of broader instructional programs and evaluate ways they might be improved. In addition, they use it in a public relations sense to inform their communities about the quality of the learning experiences being provided to their children.

Parents use assessment information to track the learning success of their children and of other students in their children's school or district in order to make decisions about how to support that success.

Next comes the community at large: Taxpayers must decide whether to support school funding, and they too consider evidence of student achievement in their evaluation process. We must not overlook political leaders: school board members and legislators. Their support for school funding and instructional priorities is often based on how they interpret evidence of student achievement.

If we are to develop truly effective schools, we must understand that these various decision makers need information about different aspects of student learning in different forms at different times to do their jobs. Some seek to support learning, others to judge its sufficiency; some need detailed information, others summary information; some need assessment results frequently, while for others annually is frequent enough. Clearly, no single assessment can meet the diverse informational needs of all these users—especially those that come only once a year. In order to meet such a wide range of informational needs, an effective local school district assessment system or program must include a variety of assessments. A few may be externally imposed standardized tests, but the majority will be developed or selected and used day to day in the classroom by teachers and their students.

## WHAT WE ASSESS

Here again, we find considerable complexity. But it is essential that we confront that complexity if we are to understand why achievement standards provide the foundation of good assessment.

As it turns out, we expect our students to achieve in many different ways. Look at any list of school district, state, or federal achievement standards and you will see that students are expected to gain *content knowledge,* to be able to *reason and figure things out,* to master *performance skills,* to create *products* that meet certain standards of quality, and develop important *attitudes, beliefs,* and *values.* These labels represent only the beginning. Hang onto your hat as we enumerate the multitude of learning targets we expect teachers to deliver and students to hit within each of those categories. Bear in mind that teachers must not only teach these things but must also be ready to assess each of them.

To begin with, there's *content knowledge*, both in the form of discrete facts and complex processes and ideas, and across all school subjects. These days, teachers must differentiate between content students are expected to learn outright and things they must know how to retrieve when they need it through reference sources (including online sources). Students' structures of knowledge grow and become increasingly integrated and differentiated as grade level increases. If a teacher is to manage these learning progressions and know what comes next in any individual student's learning, that teacher must be able to assess where the student is now in that learning.

Moving on to *reasoning and problem solving* proficiencies, where we expect students to use their knowledge to figure things out, each school subject brings its own reasoning targets for teachers and students—math problem solving, scientific inquiry, reading comprehension, composition of original text, and so on. As grade level increases and students master ever deeper and more differentiated content frameworks, the complexity of the problems they are called upon to solve increases. Teachers need to be masters of the patterns of reasoning in the subjects they teach, and they must be prepared to assess the achievement of their students as they master those patterns.

Continuing, *performance skills* ask students to master certain behavioral capabilities: vocal or instrumental music, dramatic performance, foreign language fluency, physical education, oral reading fluency, speech, technical skills ranging from photography to woodworking to computer use, and so on. In this case, the proficient learner must be able to demonstrate the skill in question so his or her teacher can observe the performance and evaluate quality.

Further, in virtually every academic discipline, teachers expect students to use their knowledge, reasoning, and performance skills to create *products* that are of high quality: multi-genre research papers, films, musical compositions, artistic projects, computer displays or games, science models, and so on. Again, teachers must develop criteria for judging the quality of such products.

But our aspirations for our children don't stop here. We want them to become confident, independent, lifelong learners. The rapid changes in our culture and correspondingly complex workplace demands require these capabilities. We want them to be prepared to communicate flexibly and effectively, collaborate productively, solve problems creatively, and eventually, take control of their own learning and set goals for themselves.

In short, teachers face an enormously demanding task. Depending on the instructional context, a teacher needs to be ready to evaluate the quality of student performance in a multitude of achievement and dispositional domains. In any particular classroom, a teacher may need to accommodate a wide range of student achievement in these various domains. Doing this well, and adjusting to fluctuating demands, takes careful training and practice, especially when it comes to assessment.

## HOW WE ASSESS

The good news is that assessors have a limited array of assessment methods from which to choose when gauging student mastery. Here are the choices—and there are no others:

- multiple choice tests
- essay or written response assessment
- performance assessment (observe and judge it)
- direct personal interaction (ask students questions and listen to their answers)

None of these methods is inherently superior to any other, but each method brings strengths and weaknesses that make it preferable in particular contexts. It is essential that teachers receive training in choosing a proper method for a particular context. The majority of teachers have not received that training.

One of the major shortcomings of assessment in American schools over the past century has been our almost obsessive reliance on multiple choice testing, regardless of context. When test development begins with an a priori decision to rely solely on multiple choice items, the range of learning targets that can be assessed is severely restricted. The only targets well-assessed with a multiple choice format are discrete, disconnected elements of knowledge (one per test item) and some simple patterns of reasoning, such as comparative reasoning or classification.

The question we should be asking our school leaders and the testing community is, are there no complex interconnected structures of knowledge, complex patterns of reasoning, performance skills, or product development capabilities we care about deeply and include in our curricula? Of course, there are. Do our high-stakes accountability annual standardized multiple choice tests assess them? Not if they rely only on that format—and most have done so for decades.

## HOW WE COMMUNICATE RESULTS

Even if we develop and use a high quality assessment, if the results are not communicated effectively to the intended user, that assessment is wasted. Communication is judged to be successful if the message sender formulates and delivers it in a manner which results in clear and complete understanding by the receiver. Only then can that person act on those results productively.

Given this overarching goal, the keys to effective communication in any particular assessment context are a function of the manner in which a test is being used. For example, if the purpose is to inform a summary judgment about the sufficiency of a student's learning success, then the results need to help the message receiver understand which of the achievement standards assessed he or she did and did not master. If communication takes the form of a test score or a letter grade, then proper interpretation requires that the recipient understand the specific relationship between the letters or numbers used and the achievement standards they are intended to represent. If this understanding is missing, miscommunication or at least inadequate communication is assured and productive action may remain beyond reach.

However, if the purpose of the assessment is to inform decisions intended to guide future student learning, as in formative assessment applications, then the communication needs to help the learner understand how to do better the next time. This requires a narrower focus and descriptive detail as the student advances step-by-step through the prerequisite learning targets leading to mastery of the achievement standard in question. In this case, the message receiver is the student, so the feedback must reveal to the learner what comes next in the learning. If this insight is not successfully delivered or inferred, the chances of ongoing learning success for the student are greatly reduced.

Both reasons for communicating effectively are important: to support learning and to certify or verify it. But they are different in the requirements they place on the communicator. Clearly, effective communication of assessment results depends on the assessors' understanding of and ability to adjust for purpose.

## CONSIDER THE CONSEQUENCES

The assessment challenges faced by any assessor in any instructional context should be clear now. Whether designing an international, national, state, local, or day-to-day classroom assessment, in order to assess effectively, the user must work systematically through a series of questions, the answers to which will define that particular context. Those questions are summarized in Table 1.

| **Table 1** | Design Decisions That Define the Realm of Educational Assessment |
| --- | --- |

---

*In this particular assessment context:*

---

*Why am I assessing student learning?*

    For formative reasons to support learning?

    For summative reasons to judge the sufficiency of learning?

*What am I assessing by way of student learning?*

    Mastery of content knowledge?

    Ability to use knowledge to reason and figure things out?

    Development of performance skills?

    Mastery of product development capabilities?

    Development of affective dispositions?

*Given the purpose and learning target, how therefore should I assess?*

    Multiple choice?

    Essay or written response?

    Performance assessment?

    Personal interaction or communication?

*How should I communicate results to the intended user(s)?*

    In sufficient detail and with sufficient frequency to support ongoing learning?

    As a summary judgment regarding mastery of required material?

---

A poor decision at any point in this sequence can spell disaster for the learner. Imagine the dire consequences for that learner if, in their particular context—

- The assessor is so unclear about the reason for the assessment that a standardized test or classroom assessment is used that is incapable of delivering the results needed to inform pending decisions, or
- Learning targets are so unclear that the assessor selects a wrong assessment method leading to the systematic mismeasurement of achievement, or
- Their teacher is not trained to develop the quality assessment exercises and scoring schemes needed to generate the results needed to help a child, or
- The results of tests used take the form of a score, the meaning or implications of which are unclear to those who are to act on it.

If this is what's going on in classrooms, learners are suffering due to inept assessment. Now let me describe for you what that suffering looks like in the learning life of a real student. The stories I am about to share reveal the personal side of our assessment problems and the solution to those problems.

# 3  Understanding Our Assessment Trap

*The illiterate of the future will not be those who cannot read.*
*It will be the person who does not know how to learn.*

Alvin Toffler

I failed reading in third grade, and the implications of this early failure turned out to be far-reaching and long lasting. I was the poster boy for struggling learners in school during those years. Ultimately, I recovered, but the damage done could have been prevented.

Obviously, large numbers of students continue to struggle in school just as I did. The problem of student failure represents one of our most visible social priorities today. In direct response, political, community, and educational leaders ask that our schools "leave no child behind." We demand that our teachers and school leaders

- narrow the achievement gap,
- lower dropout rates,
- turn out lifelong learners, and
- promote much higher levels of high school graduation.

Each of these directs our attention to struggling learners. Obviously, we do not want to narrow the achievement gap by lowering the achievement of those students doing best in our schools. These students don't drop out. They graduate on time and probably will be ready for life success. We're not leaving them behind. If we wish to comply with the above directives, the only way to do so is to help those who struggle learn more and remain in school.

At some level and for the first time, our society now demands near universal academic competence. We expect all students to become lifelong learners. Schools can no longer merely write off struggling learners as the losers in the natural competition of schooling, leaving them at the bottom of the high school rank order. Society will no longer permit its educators to dismiss our dropouts as incapable of becoming proficient readers, writers, or math problem solvers. These are the essential lifelong learner proficiencies to which we have come to believe each student is entitled. We now have national educational standards focused on these proficiencies. Educators' salaries—indeed, their very employment— now depends on their success at delivering this form of near universal learning success, as reflected on new accountability tests.

But our school improvement priorities don't stop there. Society also demands that those students doing best in our schools attain ever-higher levels of achievement, master more rigorous academic material, and attain college degrees in much higher numbers. Today, we direct our educators to make sure all students are "ready for college or workplace training programs."

Clearly, our teachers and school leaders are having difficulty delivering on these priorities. Achievement gaps are narrowing in some contexts but not in many others. Table 2 reveals that dropout rates remain scandalously high—near 25 percent of students—national test scores are not increasing, and employers continue to complain about the competence of the workforce. In short, we continue to leave lots of students behind while keeping others from their full potential.

Without question, the most powerful lesson I learned through decades in a classroom—first and always as a learner but later as a teacher and researcher—is that day-to-day classroom assessments can do more to build or to destroy students' confidence than any other schooling intervention. As it turns out, students' level of confidence links directly to how hard students try and, therefore, how much they learn.

| Table 2 | Trend in National Average Freshman Graduation Rates | | | | | | | | |
|---|---|---|---|---|---|---|---|---|---|
| *Year* | *2001–2* | *2002–3* | *2003–4* | *2004–5* | *2005–6* | *2006–7* | *2007–8* | *2008–9* | *2009–10* |
| % | 73 | 74 | 75 | 75 | 74 | 73 | 74 | 75 | 78 |

*Source:* Adapted from U.S. Department of Education (2011).

The mere act of judging student achievement and communicating test results can, if not skillfully and sensitively handled, trigger emotional dynamics within learners that stop them in their tracks, literally driving them from school. On the other hand, when handled well, assessment can launch students into powerful learning trajectories, resulting in major achievement gains for all—but especially those who have struggled to succeed.

To illustrate the difference between these two experiences from the student's point of view, let me recount two true stories from my early learning life. They juxtapose failure and success in school in a manner that reveals the changes needed in our thinking about how assessment fits into truly effective schools. Success and failure in school have both personal and academic consequences and the two interact in complex and very important ways.

## RICK CAN'T READ!

In the small town of Canandaigua in western New York, my third grade teacher was Miss G. Visualize 25 of us seated in straight rows in alphabetical order. There was Eddie A. at the head of the first row over by the windows. Next came Jim B., then Judy C., and so on. Since my name begins with an S, I was near the end of the last row—way over by the bulletin boards. Only Dave W. sat behind me, and Terry S. was just in front of me.

When the time came for instruction in reading, Miss G. would tell us to take out our reading books and open to a particular page. This was the story we were about to read aloud. She would turn to Eddie A. and nod—he knew his job was to rise from his desk, stand with proper posture, and read the first paragraph of the story aloud. When he finished, Jim B. would follow, and so we would go down the row reading the story for others to hear.

For reasons that we understand today but did not back then, I have difficulty with oral reading fluency. My eyes, brain, and mouth are not "wired" to work effectively together in this context—a reality I have accommodated successfully as an adult by avoiding any circumstance that requires reading aloud. But back then it was a big problem because avoidance was not an option. I was constantly at risk of embarrassing myself in a very public way and did so regularly. So I needed a risk management strategy—a way to minimize the embarrassment. This is the one I used, as did many others, I have since found out: I would count the number of students in class that day, count down the paragraphs to find mine, and practice reading it silently to myself. I found that if I could have a few minutes to concentrate on my passage, I could almost memorize it, and then stand and recite it, thus fooling the listeners into thinking I could read and not embarrassing myself.

One day, about halfway through the story, my strategy revealed its shortcomings when Miss G. asked a comprehension question and spontaneously called on me to answer it. I couldn't answer it—I didn't even know what the question was because I hadn't been listening. I'd been practicing. But Miss G. didn't know this, so she filed away her first piece of data for "data-based instructional decision making"—*Rick isn't getting this. . . .*

We proceeded down the rows and Terry S.—right in front of me—was reading his paragraph. As he read, fear raged within me because I was next: I had sweaty palms, and felt heart-pounding, stark terror. As Terry finished, I heard in my head the words "Rick, you're on." As I was about to rise from my desk, Miss G. actually said the worst words I could have dreamed up: "Terry you did that so beautifully and your paragraph was so short. Would you read another one for us?" The one performance I might have conquered, or at least survived, had been swept from under me. Terry, as I might have predicted, read my passage far better than I ever could have and I was compelled to try reading the next unpracticed paragraph, making a fool of myself once again.

Things like this happened quite often. My worst nightmare occurred whenever Miss G. decided to rely on what I have come to call "reading roulette," where she would call on us at random to read. I knew I would get hammered again with more public embarrassment. It was just a matter of when, and I was powerless to prevent it.

Whenever circumstances had me read without any practice—or more correctly, fail to read—Miss G. continued to gather additional pieces of achievement data. Eventually, she had enough data that she began to send notes home to my parents, saying, in essence, "Rick can't read." Now I was certainly a good enough reader to read these notes as I walked home, and I saw a serious problem brewing. Sure enough, at the end of the first grading period, there it was on my report card, right next to Reading: a great big F.

Why was it there? Two reasons: First, the F informed both me and my family that my achievement was at a low level. And given that the target being evaluated was oral reading proficiency, it conveyed an accurate message. Second—and this is important—that F was supposed to be a motivator (of the stick rather than the carrot variety)—to get me going so I would not continue to fail in the future. My Dad said it was supposed to be a kick in the pants.

Mom, Dad, and Miss G. had launched a frontal attack on this non-reader. "We know you can do it. You just have to try harder," they admonished. Nevertheless, despite all this "motivation," the second report card contained the same despair-inducing message: "Reading: F." A trajectory of failure had emerged and I wasn't at all sure I could stop it.

The next crucial decision in my academic development was mine, made privately. At some point in the progression of those "Fs," I lost hope and said to myself, "You're a non-reader. It will always be so. Get over it." I gave up in hopelessness. Do you think that was what Mom, Dad, and Miss G. wanted me to think or do? Of course not. They wanted just the opposite. The publicly reported failure was supposed to motivate me toward success, but instead I developed a deep sense of futility—I could see no path to success.

Perhaps you're thinking that in fourth grade or fifth—or surely by sixth or seventh—things somehow got better. But that isn't how it works for chronic failures who lose confidence in themselves in the classroom. I held that academic self-concept as a non-reader all the way through high school. But that wasn't the worst of it. The equally serious problem was that my sense of myself as incapable of learning didn't stop with reading. Because I didn't understand that reading aloud represented only a small part of this "reading proficiency" learning target, I concluded that *all* reading proficiency was beyond my reach. No doubt about it: The reading door was closed for me. And to make matters even worse, as I progressed through the grades, much of academic success in school hinged on reading ability. Junior high and high school were all about reading and memorizing test content for the upcoming test. I was doomed. "Not a good student" doesn't begin to describe my high school life. I had occasion to return to my high school a few years ago to receive an honor and asked if they had a copy of my transcript still on file. They did, and oh my.

Now, to be sure, I didn't have a bad life during those years. I was part of a loving family, became a pretty good athlete, and was socially adept. But none of that had anything to do with myself as a learner. Because I was sure I was incapable of learning, I didn't try, and taught myself not to care. I had no academic confidence. The mission of the high school was to rank us from highest to lowest based on achievement, and my place in the rank order of our senior class was quite low.

The reward-and-punishment-driven personal learner accountability system (the classroom testing and grading process) that was supposed to motivate productive action on my part had done just the opposite. In the win-or-lose academic competition of high school, I came to see myself as a loser. The impact of that judgment was deep and long-lasting. As my teammates took college entrance exams, I didn't bother. As they headed to university, I had no direction.

After a stint at a trade school and facing imminent draft into the Vietnam War, I enlisted in the Air Force. Things were about to turn, but before I show you how, let me highlight the point of my first story—Rick, the academic loser. Notice who was interpreting the results of my teachers' evaluative judgments and who was making the decisions that led to my poor performance. My teachers were players in the process, but *I was the driver.* True enough, my parents or teachers might have helped me to interpret things differently, to see that early failures do not define a learner for all time, or that difficulty with one sort of task does not determine ability to perform related tasks. But keep in mind that would have been in disharmony with one of the school's chief missions at the time: to grade and to rank. Generally speaking, parents of that era accepted the authority of teachers and school leaders. That leads to my second story.

## FINALLY, SOME SUCCESS

Lackland Air Force Base, Texas: After the drill instructors and basic training reset my attitudes about authority and personal responsibility, the Air Force sent me to aircraft mechanic school. It was a 15-week program of study that was divided into five 3-week units and led to an important realization—that I wasn't as stupid as I had come to believe.

Just to be clear from the outset, the mission of Air Force technical schools is not merely to produce a dependable rank order of aircraft mechanics at the end of its programs of study. Rather, every graduate had to become a highly competent mechanic or serious problems would result—especially for pilots. The Air Force technical training staff accomplished this in a manner that substantially differed from that of the traditional public school.

The first 3-week unit focused on knowledge of airplane systems. We had to know and understand engines, hydraulics, electrical systems, avionics (flight instruments), airframes, and so on. At the beginning of unit one, they told us that to pass this unit, within three weeks we had to score 75 or higher on a one hundred question multiple choice test. Then, to our surprise, on the first day of study, they gave us a copy of the final exam taken by the previous class. They told us this wasn't our exam, but ours would include different items covering the same material. Each day at the end of formal instruction, we would search that exam together as a team to find the items that addressed what we had covered that day. So important *learning* continued. For each item, we would figure out the correct answer and analyze why the incorrect options were wrong. As a result, we were able to continuously zero in on the learning targets for which we were to be held accountable and gain greater mastery of them. This helped us gain confidence as we learned more. Our instructors didn't seem surprised, explaining, "We aren't out to fool or trick you on the test. We are always up front about what's important to know, but you have to do the learning."

At the end of the unit, I took the exam and attained a near-perfect score. When I saw the score I handed the paper back, informing them that I didn't score at this level on exams—there had to have been some mistake. "No," they replied, "this is yours, and you did a great job, airman. Keep it up." That small, unprecedented piece of learning success sticks in my mind even after all these years. Unexpected as it was, it sparked a tiny glow of confidence.

During the next three weeks, we used our new knowledge to learn to diagnose problems in airplane systems. The Air Force instructors had created apparatus-based performance assessments that allowed them to induce problems in simulated hydraulic, electrical, and engine operating systems. We had to figure out what went wrong—what needed to be fixed. They showed us some of these problems and diagnoses—again, right at the beginning. Then, system by system, they helped us learn how to do what was expected. As a final exam three weeks later, they presented us with ten such systems problems to diagnose. We had to be successful on at least seven to continue. I figured out each problem and scored at the highest level on the exam. Now I was on a two-win streak, and the glow of confidence grew a little brighter.

To make a long story bearable, after fifteen weeks, every unit had unfolded for us with this kind of approach and, for me, given this kind of learning success, levels of achievement I had never experienced before. I was among the most highly-qualified graduates.

Of course, I don't tell this story to be boastful, but rather to explain how my glow of confidence became a small flame because there were learning targets I was given the opportunity to understand from the beginning and that I cared about and wanted (needed) to master. I remember beginning to realize that I might have been wrong in my early judgments about my learning ability. My turnaround was under way.

## THE TALE OF TWO LEARNERS

If we are to bring schools into the twenty-first century, in part, by weaving in truly helpful assessment systems, it is crucial that we understand the differences between these two learning experiences—the struggling reader versus the student airman—*from the learner's point of view.* We must understand these two kinds of evaluation experiences—one resulting in failure and the other in success—in terms of the emotional dynamics for the student and the resulting implications for school success.

As we proceed through this comparison, I will draw conclusions about what we, as teachers, coaches, and mentors, can do to harness productive emotional dynamics to help learners in any context overcome their failures and maximize their successes.

Poor early performance in reading aloud devolved into unfortunate personal generalizations about my overall academic ability and, ultimately, into a record of chronic low performance. In my mind I came to see failure as inevitable, and I gave up. To my mind, I had no way of controlling or even influencing my own well-being in school. Ultimately, because I failed to learn to read, I experienced low performance in most other academic contexts for a long time. As you can see, I generalized my inference that I was not a good student and never would be.

Once I had given up in early grades, the underlying truth about my learning potential no longer mattered. Even though I found out later that my elementary records included a pretty high IQ score, my actual intellectual capabilities became irrelevant. It didn't matter what my teachers believed about me. It didn't matter that Mom had confidence that I could succeed if I just tried. One of my teachers noted on one report card, "Rick seems to have a mental block to reading." Indeed.

When small measures of learning success finally began to emerge much later in Air Force tech school, my emerging confidence fueled little bits of cautious optimism that gave me the inner reserves needed to risk trying again—and this time, with a bit more energy. The result was more success, and with that success came a growing sense of internal control over my own academic well-being. Like most winning streaks, mine took on a life of its own. I entered a personal upward spiral that left my unhappy history of failure far back in the dust.

I share this analysis of my failure and success, of pessimism turned to optimism, in order to point out that powerful roadblocks to learning can arise from the very process of assessing and evaluating the performance of the learner, depending on how the learner interprets what is happening to her or him. In the next chapter we explore how and why our current assessment systems leave lots of students in their own "failing" frame of mind as they accept their own lack of hope for learning success.

# 4

# These Are Troubled Times in the Realm of Educational Assessment

*Failure is simply the opportunity to begin again, this time more intelligently.*

Henry Ford

Until the middle of the last century, society had been satisfied evaluating its schools based on the quality of the instruction provided. The implicit assumption was that if good teaching was provided, the achievement outcomes would take care of themselves. However, that confidence was shaken in the 1950s and 1960s, by social upheaval at home and the space race with the Soviet Union, beginning with the USSR's launch of the first satellite, Sputnik. We began to ask serious questions about the quality of our schools, and this spawned a desire to evaluate them based on actual achievement results. Those in positions of civic leadership came to believe we could base that evaluation on evidence derived from annual standardized tests and, in doing so, we could improve the quality of our schools. What follows is a brief history of the implications of that naïve belief.

My purpose in reviewing this history is not to challenge annual accountability testing or advocate for its removal. This testing strategy, in fact, has had little impact on instruction for several reasons. We must understand that its lack of influence does not arise from the inappropriateness of the tests, but rather the insufficiency of the information they provide. We have relied on them too heavily when we should have been supplementing them with other applications of assessment that can provide the additional evidence needed to improve student learning.

There are those who would contend that we never expected our annual standardized tests to do the school improvement job by themselves. But, in fact, this is the only application of assessment in which we have invested. As the development of annual standardized tests outlined below will reveal, the investment has been immense. If we had believed that other applications of assessment could help improve schools—such as day-to-day classroom assessment—would we not have invested as heavily in their quality, development, and use? Clearly, we have not done that. Training programs for teachers and school leaders have remained devoid of any helpful classroom assessment training. We have not even invested in preparing practitioners to use the standardized tests we have banked on so heavily. Neither our evaluations of the quality of teaching and teacher performance nor our evaluations of school leaders have ever included an examination of the quality of their assessment practices. Until very recently, as a society we have invested in only one vision of excellence in assessment in our schools. Let's take a look at that history.

Our story begins with college admissions tests. From the 1950s we have been led to believe they predict academic success and so have made them the gatekeeper for access to our system of higher education. If fact, they provide only a very modest prediction of freshman grade point average and do not predict GPA beyond the first year. High school grades are as predictive as these test scores, yet as a society, we rarely question the lofty status of SAT scores.

In the 1950s and 1960s, in response to the growing demand for more effective schools, local school boards adopted district-wide standardized testing programs to compare the scores of their schools to national norms. The resulting test scores were reported in the local media in the hope that this would promote school improvement. It did not matter that local educators had little idea what was being covered on these published tests or how those expectations related to their local curriculum; they had absolutely no training in how to interpret technically complex scores, let alone how to use tests to improve schools.

In recounting this history of the "accountability movement," allow a cash register to ring up in your mind accumulating the long-term costs. Each new level of testing was added on to those that preceded it. Again, my intent is not to use this as an argument to stop the testing. Rather, it is to reveal why these testing practices have done so little to promote instructional improvement.

In the 1960s, we began ranking states based on average college admissions test scores and reporting the results in the news media, assuming that low ranking states would be sufficiently concerned that they would work harder to improve their schools. However, those mandating such rankings had no idea that few educators had any idea what was tested on college admissions tests or, indeed, whether what was tested could be influenced by improved instruction. Indeed, these were referred to as tests of scholastic aptitude and the conventional wisdom was that this student characteristic could not be improved with study. Regardless, the mere fact of the public reporting of those relative test score ranks was considered sufficient to drive school improvement.

In the 1970s, we added state-wide testing programs. We began that decade with very few state-wide testing programs and ended the decade with programs in the majority of states. Surely, those in leadership positions believed, if we compare local districts' performance with each other and report the results to the public, districts will work harder to be sure their schools improve.

In the 1970s and 1980s, we added a national assessment program. Education leaders adopted and began testing a common set of achievement expectations so we could compare states on student performance with the intent of helping low performing states. The ranking of states has remained quite stable.

In the 1990s we became enamored of international testing programs comparing nations, and the United States finished in the middle of the pack. Surely, political and school leaders announced, we can and should do better. We were (and are) embarrassed and that should begin to improve things, they hoped. Again, it did not matter that few at the local level had any idea what was tested or, therefore, knew how to improve instruction in the service of greater success. Our place in the rank order of countries remains essentially unchanged.

In the 2000s, political pressures gave rise to our first-time-ever, national, every-pupil testing in the service of "leaving no child behind," as control over the accountability movement and its drive to promote better schools completed its journey from local school boards to state legislatures and on to the federal government.

More recently, we see a movement to attach teachers' and administrators' salaries and employment status to changes revealed in annual standardized test scores. Once again, it appears that those setting such policies are unaware of the fact that most teachers teach at grade levels and in subjects where no standardized test is available and, even when they are, these annual accountability tests:

- have not been designed or validated for this purpose,
- often do not align with an individual teacher's assigned teaching responsibilities,
- are not sensitive enough to detect the impact of an individual teacher on these test scores, and
- yield scores that are influenced by many factors that are beyond the control of teachers.

In short, they cannot serve productively in this capacity.[1]

Once a layer of testing was added, it remained. All the layers remain in place today, with another half a billion dollars currently being spent to create and implement new Common Core Standards in national tests. Seven decades later, the time has arrived to reflect on and talk about the cost of this intervention—in terms of time and money—in relation to its contribution to school improvement. In some instances, students can spend as many as 30 or 40 instructional days or more of a 180-day school year taking tests.

Despite this enormous investment of time and money, scores on our national examinations have changed little, achievement gaps have not narrowed as fast as we would like, our place in international rankings remains fairly static, dropout rates remain unacceptably high, and graduation rates remain unacceptably low. Surely, there are many causes contributing to these outcomes, but as we reflect on causes, it is relevant to ask, *Has annual testing delivered on its promise of improved schools, especially at a level commensurate with its costs?*

When school improvement researchers develop new instructional ideas, they are expected to carry out rigorous scientific studies to demonstrate that implementation of their intervention will enhance student learning. They are expected to demonstrate the impact of their teaching idea by showing how much better students perform once the new approach is in place. In school improvement research circles, this has become the coin of the realm for defending new ideas. I can find no place where this often-demanded scientific research has even been proposed, let alone conducted for standardized testing. Think about what this says about our blind faith in the utility of these tests.

Some will contend that these tests are not supposed to be the *cause* of school improvement. Rather, their intended purpose is to measure the *effects* of school improvement interventions. But when we witness the immense costs associated with this practice, I must don my taxpayer hat. We should demand evidence that this has been a sound investment of our educational tax dollars. Without this kind of cost/benefit analysis, how do we judge value in relation to other school improvement alternatives? Rather than using the absence of this research to argue for ending the testing, we should use it to understand the limits of this form of testing and, thus, to keep its expected benefits in perspective. Our assessment resources should be allocated across assessment strategies or applications in proportion to the expected contributions to school improvement.

## THE CAUSES OF OUR TROUBLED TIMES

This brief retrospective alludes to some of the reasons for our chronic inability to connect testing to instructional improvement. They arise from the professional environment that has surrounded assessment practices over the decades. Let me spell out those causes explicitly and in some detail. They define both the reasons for our decades of assessment discontent and the remedies needed to create a new and productive vision of excellence in assessment of our schools.

### Lack of Assessment Expertise

In recent decades, annual test scores have often been delivered to local teachers and administrators who are unschooled in what is being tested, what the scores mean, how to interpret them, and how to link them to instructional decisions, but it does not stop there.

As shocking as it may seem, very few teachers and even fewer school administrators have been trained to use the assessment process productively to promote learning—whether standardized tests or day-to-day classroom assessments. That's right: *Despite the fact that the typical teacher will spend a quarter to a third of her or his professional time involved in assessment-related activities and school administrators are charged with making key program decisions based on assessment results, typically, college preparation programs for each remain devoid of relevant, instructionally-helpful assessment training.* Sound absurd? Of course it is. This would be akin to training physicians to practice medicine without teaching them what lab tests to request for their patients or how to interpret the results of such tests.

In Chapter 5, we will review the specific competencies an assessment literate classroom teacher should have mastered to teach effectively, but for now, let us just consider the implications of this particular lack of professional competence. This means that day-to-day classroom assessments of student achievement may very often yield undependable results, leading to the misrepresentation of each student's actual learning. It would render report card grades meaningless. Further, it would result in teachers frequently misdiagnosing student learning needs. And because school leaders lack sufficient classroom assessment expertise, teachers have no place to turn for assessment help if and when they need or want it. This is simply an unacceptable state of affairs.

## Lack of Leadership Vision

Another reason for the educational blindness inherent in our testing practices has been the naiveté about testing practices among those in positions of political and community leadership. In their defense, they are doing the best they can in light of the scant information provided to them. Often they are advised by practitioners unschooled (as we have seen) in how to link testing to teaching and learning. This has resulted in the testing layers spelled out above—local to state to national to international applications—that have, in effect, shifted our thinking about assessment farther and farther from the classroom. Indeed, the day-to-day classroom level of assessment, including teacher developed or textbook embedded tests (the other 99 percent of the assessments that happen in a student's life), is almost always missing from the list of interventions that can improve schools. This is because the policy makers who set assessment practice at federal, state, and local levels have rarely been given opportunities to learn about testing and learning. If such opportunities were to be forthcoming, the first lesson we would teach them is that assessments occurring only once a year are not likely to be of much value to those making instructional decisions every three to four minutes.

## The Measurement Community

Often, the testing professionals who carry out the development of our large-scale, high-stakes standardized assessments have been expected to understand little about the instructional realities that exist within schools and classrooms. It has not been their job to appreciate the difficulties of trying to create an assessment when you have no idea where to start, or trying to create an assessment of a learning target you yourself have not mastered, or adding ever more learning targets to an already overcrowded curriculum, or searching for ways to motivate students who feel overwhelmed, or wondering how to present new skills in reading, writing, or math when there are simply no minutes left in the day. With a few exceptions, testing professionals have little training in, awareness of, or concern for how their assessments could directly drive or influence student learning day to day in the classroom.

Members of the measurement community tend to fall into one of three subgroups: test publishers, psychometricians in academic settings, or testing practitioners at state or local levels. The first group's business interest resides in complying with (not questioning) the testing demands of those policy makers who pay them for their testing services. Those concerned with psychometrics deal with the technical complexities of large-scale test score quality—their validity and reliability. While these standards of quality make sense to them in that context, translating them for classroom application is not their job. Local assessment specialists typically face and must deal with the accountability pressures of their state department of education and local school board. This has left little time to deal with assessment in the context of actual teaching and learning.

## Lack of Collaboration

Further, the various players in the accountability testing realm—policy makers, the professional testing community, and practitioners—tend not to collaborate in the promotion of productive assessment in the improvement of our schools. If (a) teachers and school leaders have been given little opportunity to understand the basic principles of sound assessment practice, (b) policy makers and the testing experts who drive testing practice have little sense of day-to-day life in classrooms, and (c) there are no natural ways for these groups to interact, how could we expect collaboration? How could assessment possibly serve to improve day-to-day instruction and student learning?

## Role of the News Media

Most often, the link between school leaders who have test scores to report and the public in need of that information is the news media. So, if a report is issued linking some student characteristic, schooling practice, or instructional activity to test scores, reporters—many of whom, once again, are not trained to evaluate the evidence provided—send it unquestioned out into the community. They take the evidence on faith. But what if that faith is not justified; what if the evidence is unsound? What if it misrepresents actual student achievement? Again, as with policy makers and practitioners, reporters have rarely had the opportunity to learn what questions to ask in this regard or how to evaluate the answers they receive.

## No Wonder . . .

Through decades of increasing demand for layer upon layer of ever-higher annual test scores, why have we expressed so little concern about the impact of our assessment practices on actual day-to-day teaching, learning, and student success? How do you build a dependable assessment system for local districts, schools, and classrooms when so few of those involved understand the intricacies of assessment, the subtleties of classroom instruction, the dynamics of learning, and how to blend them productively? As important as these questions are, they represent just the tip of this iceberg. What if—

- the tests in which we have invested so heavily happen too infrequently (say, only once a year) to inform the far more frequent instructional decisions that really drive school quality and student learning success?

- the tests are too expansive in scope yet too shallow in coverage to provide depth of evidence needed to improve instruction day to day in the classroom?
- the test format (say, multiple choice items) cannot reflect the more complex learning targets local communities are demanding in twenty-first century schools?
- the timing of test administration during the instructional year is wrong—for example, testing things before they have even been taught?
- because of differences of local opinion about what is important, or because of insufficient local resources, that which is tested is not given priority attention by local teachers, parents, and curriculum guidelines?

## THE TIME FOR REEVALUATION IS AT HAND

Compare the assessment environment described above with that reflected in another nation's expression of its assessment priorities. *Directions for Assessment: New Zealand,* a policy statement on this topic from the Ministry of Education, opens with this paragraph:

> Given the extent of change in the educational landscape over recent years, it is appropriate that we reconsider the purposes for which we assess and the processes by which we pursue these purposes. In doing so . . . we identify a priority that ranks above all others: strengthen the *assessment capabilities of students* by enhancing the assessment capabilities of their teachers, school leaders, parents and those who support them. (Absolum, et al., 2009, p. 1, emphasis added)

In Canada, this statement of intent from the British Columbia Ministry of Education's 2013 comprehensive education plan, titled *STUDENTS Must Be at the CENTRE of THEIR Learning,* expresses similar ideas about assessment:

> Effective *classroom assessment practices* are key to student success and will be even more vital in a more personalized learning environment. Educators will have more ability to decide how and when each student is assessed. New tools will be

developed to provide greater access, richer information, and more consistency across the province on student progress. Regular reporting to parents both formally and informally will remain key. (p. 4, emphasis added)

These school leaders are headed in a different assessment direction, one in which assessment is viewed as a teaching and learning tool—far more than a tool for public accountability.

It is time for the United States to conduct a vigorous national, state, and local inquiry into the current state of our assessment affairs. Those who have been responsible for the development and perpetuation of the current state of affairs are, of course, not in a position to lead such an inquiry, as that would represent a conflict of interest for them. Rather, the families of students currently in school, taxpayers, and those responsible for the quality of local schools (teachers and school leaders), as well as uninvolved academics with appropriate expertise, must conduct this inquiry. Judgments about the efficacy of our current system should be made by those served by that system rather than those who organize it.

Our "assessment emperor" has been scantily clad at best for decades. We understand more today than ever before about the key characteristics of a truly productive assessment system. The situation calls for a fundamental redefinition of assessment's role in our schools—it can and must both support student learning and certify it. In the chapters that follow, we will consider the new ideas, changing assumptions, and innovative practices that can drive such a new balanced vision, one which offers a role for annual accountability testing, interim benchmark assessments, and productive day-to-day classroom assessment. As we go, we will review what research tells us about how to use assessment practices to improve student learning rather than merely monitor it.

## ENDNOTE

1. I have addressed this topic directly in *Defensible Teacher Evaluation: Student Growth Through Classroom Assessment* (Stiggins, 2014).

# 5

# A New School Mission Demands a New Assessment Vision

*Tell me and I forget. Teach me and I remember. Involve me and I learn.*

Benjamin Franklin

Over the past twenty years our society has redefined the role of the social institution we call school, and, as a result, we must redefine how we use assessments of student learning. Through most of the last century, because of our social and economic circumstances, one primary mission of schools was to rank students based on their academic record—that is, to begin sorting them into the various segments of our social and economic system. Some students were destined to succeed early and often, and ultimately ride success to a high finish in the distribution of achievement, while others would fall further and further behind and, if they didn't drop out altogether, wind up occupying places low in the ranking. The greater the differences among students teachers could create using their testing and grading practices, the more dependable the rank order would be. Let me explain how this works.

Students enter first grade and, at the end of that year, some are seen to have learned a great deal and others not so much. They go on to second grade, where those who learned a lot in first grade continue their pace of learning and those who missed the first grade foundations cannot build upon them and so are doomed to learn less in second grade than they otherwise might have, and certainly less than those for whom that foundation is solid. As a result, the differences among students widen.

And so it goes for twelve years, all the way through high school, with differences among students and the spread of achievement growing each year. In the end, every student is to have found her or his place, or, to put it bluntly, will have given up along the way in the face of steep competition. Either way, the institution fulfills its assigned mission to sort us based on overall achievement.

In this sense, society based the institution of public school on the belief that we derive greatest benefit from our education dollars by investing them in our most successful learners. The least successful learners, including dropouts and those who stayed but finished low in the rank order, would merely be launched into the adult world labeled low achievers, having gained a modicum of skills viewed as sufficient to perform manual labor or in blue-collar jobs.

Assessments were structured to support this mission. Their role was to provide the evidence needed to assure that the rank order was dependable—that is, provided an accurate reflection of the underlying achievement reality. Assessments—especially college admissions tests—typically were designed to highlight differences in student learning. They were designed to compare students to one another and stretch them along an achievement continuum. Items selected for inclusion discriminated among levels of achievement for this purpose. Timed tests factored speed of response into the equation as another sorting variable, thus adding to the dependability of the rank order.

Under this model, first we teach and then we assess to evaluate learning success. If the student did not master the material, instruction moved on anyway in order to assure coverage of the content for those who could keep up with the pace. We believed this competitive classroom environment carried with it the benefit of providing a compelling motivational force for student learning. By asking students to compete for an artificial scarcity of success (as if only a limited amount could be awarded), society believed that even students who were falling behind in the race would redouble their efforts and learn more. If they did not, the personal cost to them would be very high—much higher for many, it turns out, than we anticipated.

As the new millennium approached, this unitary sort-and-select mission began to reveal its limitations. Over the last two decades of explosive evolution in technological complexity and socio-economic diversity, it became increasingly clear that certain academic proficiencies were essential for the ongoing survival of all students, not just those at the top of the rank order. Those who lacked essential lifelong learner proficiency in reading, writing, or math problem solving, for example, would not be able to keep up with the rapid pace of societal change and would not be able to survive in, let alone contribute to the development of, our nation and world.

In response, a second responsibility was added to the mission of sorting: universal competence in certain achievement domains. That is, educators were charged with helping all students attain a foundation of lifelong literacy and numeracy. In short, educators were (and are) to raise the lowest level of acceptable achievement to certain standards of academic excellence in key achievement domains such as reading and math.

This evolution of our school mission took many years and many forms, and it was assigned many labels as it emerged, the most visible of which asserted that schools must strive to "leave no child behind." Today, we see frequent reference in the media to the need to make sure that all students are ready for college or the workplace.

However, we must understand that this does not mean that all students come out of school as cookie cutter copies of each other, all shooting for the same academic and professional goals. The original mission of sorting remains in place. That means students will differ in the range and number of standards they ultimately master due to differences in ability, interests, available family resources, and emerging educational goals. Those differences will continue to be reflected in a dependable rank order by the end of high school. It is just that society is now saying that, on their way to being sorted, all students are entitled to mastery of the basic reading, writing, and math problem solving proficiencies that underpin the ability to live productively in a rapidly changing digital age.

This new priority (universal lifelong learner competence) brings with it an important potential for old/new mission conflict. Under the previous purely competitive sort-and-select mission, if some students started losing and gave up in hopelessness, their reduced investment of time and energy simply contributed to fulfillment of the schools' first mission: to rank students along a continuum of learning. Now, if some students gave up in hopelessness before attaining those essential proficiencies, schools failed in effect to fulfill their second mission: making sure all students master certain competencies. Result? Mission conflict and a dilemma.

In fact, over the past twenty years, researchers around the world have learned a great deal about how to balance assessment applications in ways that address this problem. Some of those were illustrated in the story about my training in the military as an aircraft mechanic—clear targets from the beginning, constant tracking of learning success with ongoing assessment during the learning, student self-assessment, and so on. These assessment applications center on helping learners maintain the belief that success is within reach if they keep trying. I will add more specifics about these strategies as we go, but first, let's delve more deeply into the emotional dynamics of the assessment experience and learning from the student's point of view. Or to put it another way, let's consider how being evaluated affects one's chances of learning success.

## THE EMOTIONAL DYNAMICS OF BEING EVALUATED

Permit me a personal digression. I am an avid angler, and my scrapbook of fly fishing memories and adventures opens on page one with this quotation, from Scottish poet John Buchan: "The charm of fly fishing is that it is the pursuit of what is elusive but attainable—a perpetual series of occasions for hope."

We anglers are optimists by nature, and we expect to succeed. If we do not, it is not because of failed technique but rather because there were no fish present where we tried. This confidence comes from the experience of success. At about age four my angler Dad began to teach me how to catch fish. Had I not experienced some instances of early success, I am sure I would have given up in frustration and not pursued this pastime.

My definition of angling success has evolved far beyond merely catching more fish. Rather, I succeed when I master a new technique, figure out how to catch a species not targeted before, or discover how to succeed on new water, with success always evidenced by catching fish. But the fun actually is in the learning—one beauty of fly fishing is that there is always something new to master. But I don't learn what works unless and until it actually does work. The more I succeed the more I learn.

This lesson extends far beyond angling: the beauty of learning is that it is the pursuit of something that is elusive but attainable—a constant array of occasions for hope. In all learning contexts as in angling, hope hinges on the experience of success at learning. The belief that success is possible is critical, and any teacher will tell you that the hardest student to reach is the one who says, "I just can't write," or read, or do math. If that success is not forthcoming—if failure to learn dominates in the mind of the learner—a sense of futility can take over, persistence will fade, and the learning will stop.

It's important to learn early in life that satisfaction and fulfillment arise from accomplishing what one sets out to do. Failure to achieve what we aspire to spawns dissatisfaction and frustration. However, under certain circumstances, the effect of failure can extend far beyond mere dissatisfaction to a generalized sense of defeat and hopelessness. Chronic failure defeats hope. When chronic failure besets an aspiring learner at any level, improvement slows or stops.

Given this dynamic, we must realize that the difference between success and failure hangs not only on a teacher's judgment about the level of one's performance, but also on the criteria we ourselves choose to apply in judging the quality of that performance. We must understand that those criteria can be and often are developed and applied not only by external judges (teachers, coaches, supervisors) but by the performers themselves—those who must act on the results of the evaluation in order to improve. And this happens for them *while they are learning.* It is part of what promotes the learning.

For example, athletes continuously evaluate their own performance in terms of the criteria they have in their minds and, based on their own judgments of how fast they run or how high they fly, they decide whether to (a) persevere, learn a new approach, practice harder, and improve, or, (b) give up and move on to some other activity. Students consider their current level of achievement in relation to what is being expected of them and decide whether learning success is within reach for them—that is, whether it is worthwhile to continue trying. In each of these decision contexts, the criteria that count the most are those that are understood and held to be important *by the performer*. Even though the coach might urge the athlete onward or the teacher might try to intimidate the student into further efforts with the threat of a low grade, ulti- mately, the performer's internal sense of whether he or she can con- trol the variables that ultimately will determine his or her success will rule the day. If the student believes she cannot write or read aloud or jump a four-foot hurdle, then it matters little what the external judge believes or does. True internal hopelessness trumps external pressure or encouragement. No measure of imploring, intimidation, or attempts to embarrass can restore hope if it truly has been lost. In fact, inept attempts to intimidate or embarrass typ- ically backfire and drive the hopeless deeper into despair.

What, then, is the coach, teacher, or mentor to do to encour- age success? Their job is to do *whatever they can* to convince the performer that success is within reach if she or he keeps trying. The decision about whether or not to strive is the performer's, and only the performer's, to make. But supporters can help them by, for example—

- Making sure that, as adult teachers and judges, they them- selves are confident, competent masters of the very specific criteria by which they are evaluating the performance of others;
- Helping the performer understand those criteria sufficiently well to be able to judge his or her own performance as it improves, whether running a 100-meter dash or learning to read or write (this is important because students are going to judge their own performance anyway as they grow—bet- ter that they base that judgment on the most significant cri- teria students and teachers can identify together);
- Helping performers see, understand, and remain aware of what they do well now and yet identify and accurately esti- mate the gap between where they are now and where they want to be;

- Helping performers subdivide that gap into manageable increments (this is essential to putting success constantly within reach, thereby keeping optimism high);
- Helping performers to recognize their own strengths and achievements, so they can understand how that gap is narrowing over time (this too promotes optimism, confidence, and hope).

By applying these strategies consistently, coaches, teachers, and mentors can put their charges on winning streaks and, hopefully, keep them there. To be supportive, teachers must be merchants of hope. The great Duke University basketball coach, Mike Krzyzewski, is said to have pointed out that the key to winning is not losing twice in a row. Lose once and recover with a win and you remain confident, but lose twice and confidence can be shaken, opening the door to a potential losing streak, pessimism, and declining effort.

My Air Force training experience appeared to be designed with this reality in mind. The instructors made the learning targets clear from day one of instruction. There was no need to try to guess what counted; they showed us at the outset how our achievement would be evaluated and allowed us many practice runs. Each of these was either a small win that built confidence or a loss that we turned around immediately. That enabled us to see the gap narrowing between where we were and where we knew we had to be. That awareness, in turn, gave us a laser focus on what areas of study we needed to master at any point in time to ensure our ultimate success.

When I was struggling to learn to read, the assessment process was used merely to judge and grade my performance. There was no vision of myself advancing along a continuum of learning, nor were incremental goals provided that seemed within my grasp. I had but one big goal—to become a reader—but within a short time, I was fully convinced it was out of reach, then and forever. In the Air Force, assessment served first to support learning while it was occurring and later to certify our competence when learning was to have been completed. What a difference that made.

As teachers in any context, whether the learners are our children, students, athletes, or co-workers, our success hinges on the ability to help our charges understand the gap between where they are now and where they want to be. They must believe that they can close that gap. If they stop believing this, they will cease making an effort, and they will stop the learning. In this sense, it is always the learner who is in charge of the learning.

The essence of this dynamic is most clearly understood by contrasting the internal mental experience of learners who are on winning streaks—for whom learning is unfolding over time in productive ways—and those who are on losing streaks. These students live in fundamentally different emotional worlds in terms of what assessment results say, the likely effect of those results on them, what they are likely to be thinking as they face those results, and therefore, what actions they are likely to take, and the likely effect of those actions. Table 3 compares these two emotional worlds.

| Table 3 | Contrasting Dynamics of Two Different Assessment Experiences |
| --- | --- |

| *Students on Winning Streaks* | *Students on Losing Streaks* |
| --- | --- |
| *What assessment results provide:* | |
| Continuous evidence of success | Continuous evidence of failure |
| *Likely effect on the learner:* | |
| Hope rules; remain optimistic | Hopelessness dominates |
| Success fuels productive action | Initial panic gives way to resignation |
| *What the student is probably thinking in the face of results:* | |
| It's all good; I'm doing fine | This hurts; I'm uncomfortable here |
| See the trend? I succeed as usual | I just can't do this either . . . again |
| I want more success | I'm confused; I don't like this—help! |
| We focus on what I do well | Why is it always about what I can't do? |
| I know what to do next | Nothing I do ever seems to work |
| Move on, grow, learn new stuff | Defend, hide, get away from here |
| Feedback helps me | Feedback hurts me—scares me |
| Public success feels very good | Public failure is embarrassing |
| I can even make the difficult make sense | I can't make sense of this |

| *Students on Winning Streaks* | *Students on Losing Streaks* |
| --- | --- |
| *Actions likely to be taken by the learner:* | |
| Take risks—stretch, go for it! | Trying is too dangerous—retreat, escape |
| Seek what is new and exciting | Can't keep up—can't handle new stuff |
| Seek challenges | Seek what's easy |
| Practice with gusto | Don't practice |
| Take initiative | Avoid initiative, blame others |
| Persist | Give up |
| *Likely effect of these actions:* | |
| Lay foundations now for success later | Can't master prerequisites needed later |
| Success becomes THE reward | No success—no reward |
| Self-enhancement | Self-defeat, self-destruction |
| Positive self-fulfilling prophesy | Negative self-fulfilling prophesy |
| Extend the effort in face of difficulty | Give up quickly in face of difficulty |
| Acceptance of responsibility | Denial of responsibility |
| Make success public | Cover up failure (cheat) |
| Self-analysis tells me how to win | Self-criticism is easy given my record |
| Manageable stress | Stress remains high |
| Curiosity, enthusiasm | Boredom, frustration, fear |
| Resilience | Yielding quickly to defeat |
| Continuous adaptation | Inability to adapt |

What can we do to get learners on winning streaks and keep them there if their ultimate success depends on it? Light their confidence flame and fan it with ongoing successes. Do this and they will begin to take responsibility for their own ongoing learning success.

For that to happen, their growing confidence must be fueled by a growing sense of internal control over their own success. They must believe that they have learned something important to them and that it was their own actions that drove that success. One excellent way to ensure this feeling of control over one's own destiny is to make the learner a full partner in the assessment of his or her own learning. For starters, the learner must be given a clear vision of what success looks like from the beginning of the learning process, and this must be followed by a continuous array of self-assessments (occasions for hope) that reveal steady progress toward ultimate success. The result will be increasing confidence and a sense of personal efficacy. In the absence of these key dynamics, learning will fail, regardless of the teaching and learning context.

To explain these dynamics more clearly, I turn to Harvard professor Rosabeth Moss Kanter's 2004 book, *Confidence: How Winning and Losing Streaks Begin and End.*[1] Her book arises from her study of business and athletic team success and failure and is aimed at an audience of business leaders, but I was stunned by its applicability to other teaching and learning contexts, especially the public school classroom. Kanter analyzes the emotional dynamics in play and their effects in the presence of success or failure in any context including the corporate board room or the elementary school classroom.

> Confidence is not an artificial mental construct, solely dependent on what people decide to believe; it reflects reasonable reactions to circumstances. . . . Failure and success are not episodes, they are trajectories. They are tendencies, directions, pathways. . . . As patterns develop, streaks start to run on their own momentum, producing conditions that make further success or failure more likely. . . . On the way up, success creates positive momentum. People who believe they are likely to win are also likely to put in the extra effort at difficult moments to ensure victory. On the way down, failure feeds on itself. As performance starts running on a positive or a negative path, the momentum can be hard to stop. Growth cycles produce optimism, decline cycles produce pessimism. (Kanter, 2004, pp. 6–11)

These dynamics hold whether we're talking about elite basketball players, corporate leaders, or third graders. Kanter goes on to describe the effects of winning and losing:

> Losing streaks begin in response to a sense of failure, and failure makes people feel out of control. It is just one more step to a pervasive sense of powerlessness, and powerlessness erodes

confidence. When there are few resources or coping mechanisms for dealing with problems, people fall back on almost primitive, self-protective behavior. Nine pathologies begin to unfold, as an emotional and behavioral reaction:

- Communication decreases
- Criticism and blame increases
- Respect decreases
- Isolation increases
- Focus turns inward
- Rifts widen and inequalities grow
- Initiative decreases
- Aspirations diminish
- Negativity spreads

These behavioral tendencies are polar opposites of the characteristics that help winners win. (Kanter, 2004, pp. 97–98)

Kanter's insights are particularly applicable when thinking about the struggling learner in school:

One way to cope with losing is to reduce aspirations, to look for life satisfactions elsewhere, to say that winning or losing doesn't matter. . . . Psychologists use the term "defensive pessimism" to describe the way some people set low expectations to cope with anxiety in risky situations. This set of people is not trying to make excuses or deny responsibility, they prefer to expect failure, so as not to be totally debilitated by anxiety about whether they can meet lofty goals. . . . Pessimists are proven right so often because losing is easier than winning. And setting low aspirations means losing the will to win. . . . Powerlessness undermines resilience. . . . Self-confidence, confidence in another, and confidence in the system disappear. (Kanter 2004, pp. 107–111)

It is as if Professor Kanter has probed the mind and emotions of every struggling learner in every classroom in the United States. But what brings students to the place where they diverge either to confidence and winning or fear and losing—where they decide to assume responsibility or not? It is their interpretation of the evidence of their learning success—or lack thereof—that they receive from their teacher every day. Each student is in charge of this decision as the aftermath of each assessment event in their school lives. Herein lie the psychological underpinnings of student motivation and learning success.

Our aspiration must be to give each student a strong sense of control over her or his own academic well-being. Stanford Professor Albert Bandura (1994) refers to this sense as self-efficacy. He describes this as a continuum of a psychological state of mind. Here is his description of the positive or strong end of this scale:

> A strong sense of efficacy enhances human accomplishment and personal well-being in many ways. People with high assurance in their capabilities approach difficult tasks as challenges to be mastered rather than as threats to be avoided. Such an efficacious outlook fosters intrinsic interest and deep engrossment in activities. They set themselves challenging goals and maintain strong commitment to them. They heighten and sustain their efforts in the face of failure. They quickly recover their sense of efficacy after failures or setbacks. *They attribute failure to insufficient effort or deficient knowledge and skills which are acquirable.* They approach threatening situations with assurance that they can exercise control over them. Such an efficacious outlook produces personal accomplishments, reduces stress and lowers vulnerability . . . (p. 71, emphasis added)

If the reader will think of this continuum in terms of the student's sense of control over learning success (academic self-efficacy, if you will), it will become clear that any teacher's mission must be to move students toward this productive end of the scale. Our analysis of any successful students we know personally leads us to see them in exactly these positive/productive terms. Their record of success gives them the confidence to keep taking the rise of trying and the results are predictable.

However, when we reflect on students we know who are struggling, what comes to mind is a different profile. Though he was not speaking solely or particularly of students or the idea of academic self-efficacy as the described general psychological construct, in effect, Bandura describes those students who are in danger of giving up on themselves and, perhaps, of dropping out:

People who doubt their capabilities shy away from difficult tasks which they view as personal threats. They have low aspirations and weak commitment to the goals they choose to pursue. When faced with difficult tasks, they dwell on their personal deficiencies, on the obstacles they will encounter, and all kinds of adverse outcomes rather than concentrate on how to perform successfully. They slacken their efforts and give up quickly in the face of difficulties. They are slow to recover their sense of efficacy following failure or setbacks. *Because they view performance as deficient aptitude it does not require much failure for them to lose faith in their capabilities.* (p. 71, emphasis added)

We know how to help them. Let's consider an example.

## A CLASSROOM ILLUSTRATION

The following was told to me as a true story and is an illustration of the productive use of these emotional dynamics in an assessment process that moved a student along the Bandura continuum.

Picture yourself at an important meeting of the school board in your local school district. This is the once-a-year meeting at which the district presents the annual report of standardized test scores to the board and the media. Every year it's the same: Will scores be up or down? How will you compare to national norms? How will your district compare to others in the area?

What most present don't realize as the meeting begins is that this year, they are in for a big surprise with respect to both the achievement information to be presented and the manner of the presentation.

The audience includes a young woman named Emily,[2] a junior at the high school, sitting in the back of the room with her parents. It has been quite a year for her, unlike any she has ever experienced in school before. She also knows her parents and teacher are as proud of her as she is of herself.

The assistant superintendent begins by reminding the board and the rest of the audience that the district uses standardized tests that sample broad domains of achievement with just a few multiple choice test items. Much that we value, she points out, must be assessed using other methods, and she promises to provide an example later in the presentation.

Having set the stage, the assistant superintendent turns to carefully prepared charts depicting average student performance in each important achievement category tested. Results are summarized by grade and building, concluding with a description of how district results have changed from the year before and from previous years. As she proceeds, board members ask questions and receive clarification. Some scores are down slightly; some are up. Participants discuss possible reasons.

Having completed the first part of the presentation, the assistant superintendent explains how the district has gathered some new information about one important aspect of student achievement. As the board knows, the district has implemented a new writing program in the high school to address the issue of poor writing skills among graduates. As part of their preparation for this program, the English faculty attended a summer institute on assessing writing proficiency and integrating such assessments into the teaching and learning process. The English department was confident that this kind of professional development and program revision would produce higher levels of writing proficiency.

For the second half of the evening's assessment presentation, the high school English department faculty shares the results of their evaluation of the new writing program.

As the first step in this presentation, the English chair, Ms. Weathersby, who also happens to be Emily's English teacher, distributes a sample of student writing to the board members (with the student's name removed), asking them to read and evaluate this writing. They do so, expressing their dismay aloud as they go. One board member reports in exasperation that if these represent the results of that new writing program, the community has been had. The board member is right, as this is a pretty weak piece of work.

But Ms. Weathersby urges patience and asks the board members to be specific in stating what they don't like about this work. As the board registers its complaints, another member of the faculty records the criticisms on chart paper for all to see. The list is long, including everything from repetitiveness, to disorganization, to short, choppy sentences and disconnected ideas.

Next, the department chair distributes another sample of student writing, asking the board to read and evaluate it. This, they report, is much better. Be specific, the chair demands. What do you like about this work? They list positive aspects: good choice of words, sound sentence structure, clever ideas, and so on. Emily is ready to burst, and she squeezes her mom's hand.

The reason she's so full of pride at this moment is that this has been a special year for Emily and her classmates. For the first time ever, they became partners with their English teachers in managing their own improvement as writers. Early in the year, Ms. Weathersby (Ms. W, they all call her) made it clear to Emily that she was, in fact, not a very good writer and that just trying hard to get better was not going to be enough.

Ms. W started the year by working with students to set high writing standards, including understanding word choice, sentence structure, organization, and voice, and sharing some new "analytical scoring guides" written just for students. Each explained the differences between good and poor-quality writing in understandable ways. When Emily and her teacher evaluated her first two pieces of writing using these standards, she received low ratings.

Emily also began to study samples of writing her teacher supplied that Emily could see were very good. Slowly, she began to understand *why* they were good, and the differences between these and her work started to become clear. Ms. W began to share examples and strategies that would help Emily's writing improve one step at a time. As she practiced with these and time passed, Emily and her classmates kept samples of their old writing to compare to their new writing, and they began to build portfolios. Thus, she began to watch her own writing skills improve before her very eyes. At midyear, her parents were invited in for a conference at which Emily, not Ms. W, shared the contents of her portfolio and discussed her emerging writing skills. She shared thoughts about some aspects of her writing that had become strong and some examples of areas she still needed to work on. Now, the year was at an end and here she sat waiting for her turn to speak to the school board.

Having set the board up by having them analyze, evaluate, and compare these two samples of student work, Ms. W springs the surprise: The two pieces of writing they had just evaluated, one of poor and one of outstanding quality, were produced by the same writer at the beginning and at the end of the school year. This, she reports, is evidence of the kind of impact the new writing program is having on student writing proficiency.

Needless to say, all are impressed; however, one board member wonders aloud, "Have all your students improved in this way?"

Having anticipated the question, the rest of the English faculty joins the presentation and produces charts depicting dramatic changes in typical student performance over time, on rating scales for each of six clearly articulated dimensions of good writing. The teachers accompany their description of student performance on each scale with samples of student work illustrating various levels of proficiency.

Ms. W then informs the board that the student whose improvement has been so dramatically illustrated with the work they have just analyzed is present at this school board meeting, along with her parents. This student is ready to talk with the board about the nature of her learning experience.

Interest among the board members runs high. Emily talks about how she has come to understand the important differences between good and bad writing. She refers to differences she had not understood before, how she has learned to assess her own writing and to fix it when it doesn't "work well," and how she and her classmates have learned to talk with their teacher and each other about what it means to write well. Ms. W talks about the improved focus of writing instruction, increase in student motivation, and important positive changes in the nature of the student–teacher relationship.

A board member asks Emily if she likes to write, and she reports, "I do now!" This board member turns to Emily's parents and asks their impression of all of this. They report that they had never seen so much evidence before of Emily's achievement and most of it came from Emily herself. Emily had never been called on to lead the parent/teacher conference before, and they had no idea she was so articulate. Their daughter's pride in and accountability for achievement had skyrocketed in the past year.

As the meeting ends, it is clear to all in attendance that this two-part assessment presentation—one part from standardized test scores and one from students, teachers, and the classroom—reveals that assessment is in balance in this district. The test scores cover part of the picture and classroom assessment evidence completes the achievement picture. The accountability needs of the community are being satisfied, and the new writing program is working to improve student achievement.

The classroom assessment/instruction process Ms. W and her colleagues employed in support of Emily and her classmates is called "assessment FOR learning." We will explore this new application of classroom assessment in some detail in the next chapter, but to set the stage for that discussion, we need to address some common misconceptions about learning and cognition in the classroom.

## DEVELOPING THE ABILITY TO LEARN

This kind of ongoing classroom assessment process provides students with evidence of success or failure while they are still learning—while there's still time to do something about it—and that evidence is viewed and interpreted not only by the adults in the educational system but by students as well. It is crucial to understand that students are doing this kind of self-evaluation continuously while they are learning. Students know when they are or are not getting it. They make crucial inferences about what to expect from themselves, and they make important instructional decisions about what to do next based on those inferences. In the past half-century, we've come to understand much more about the interaction between assessments and learning: *We now know when and how to intercede in the learners' thought processes regarding their own ongoing self-assessment in ways that can keep them believing in themselves or help them recover any self-confidence they may have lost.*

The implications of this are enormous in terms of what we understand and believe about a person's sense of his or her own ability to learn. Many of us grew up believing that we were born with a hard-wired IQ—intelligence quotient—that is, a number that predetermined how much we could learn and how fast. Parents and teachers explained that this ability to learn varied widely across the population, and it was useful to understand where students fit into that distribution. Schools measured IQ and achievement, developing the concept of over- and under-achievers. Schools developed tracking programs—ability groupings—to accommodate differences. Once students were tracked, teachers, parents, and even students themselves could (often would) begin to behave in ways consistent with their place in the classroom. They became what those around them expected them to become with respect to learning.

Some, perhaps many, are still allowing early expectations to define them once and for all. It is time to stop perpetuating these self-fulfilling prophesies. It is time to update our collective understanding of these matters.

While ability to learn varies across the population, researchers have helped us understand that such ability is not a stable human characteristic. Rather, it can be developed (improved) throughout the course of one's lifetime—and it can also decline or even atrophy, if tamped down or left uncultivated. Improvement turns on (a) the learner's beliefs about her or his own intelligence, and (b) the quality of the learning environment available to the learner. With respect to the former, the learner needs to be confident that he or she can get better at learning. The learning environment, in turn, must encourage the student to learn, as well as providing evidence of successful learning in order to keep confidence levels high.

The only way to promote and maintain self-confidence is to help the learner experience success that occurs as a direct result of his or her own efforts. As Bandura contended, if "they view insufficient performance as deficient aptitude it does not require much failure for [learners] to lose faith in their capabilities."

The upper ranges of our achievement may be limited by biology; however, our ability to reach our fullest potential is limited only by our belief in ourselves. Increasing self-confidence based on evidence is precisely the method employed so successfully by the Air Force. That happened because the teachers delineated learning targets, helped students understand how to reach these, provided students with continuous evidence of their progress toward success, and then certified competence. They did this because it was their mission to promote and attain universal competence.

Parents and educators can create this same kind of self-confidence, and by doing so, can transform children's lives. They have only to recognize that the ability to learn is a changeable human characteristic, and that we hold in our hands the power to launch our students into a rapidly changing world with the capabilities needed to remain successful throughout their lives.

## ENDNOTES

1. Excerpts from *Confidence: How Winning Streaks and Losing Streaks Begin and End* by Rosabeth Moss Kanter, copyright © 2004, 2006 by Rosabeth Moss Kanter. Used by permission of Crown Business, an imprint of the Crown Publishing Group, a division of Random House LLC. All rights reserved.
2. The story about Emily is adapted from Stiggins, R. J.; Chappuis, J., *An Introduction to Student-Involved Assessment for Learning*, 6th Edition, © 2012. Adapted by permission of Pearson Education, Inc., Upper Saddle River, NJ.

# 6

# Assessment for Truly Effective Schools Requires Local School District Leadership

*Management is doing things right. Leadership is doing the right thing.*

Peter Drucker

The time has come to bring educational assessment into the twenty-first century. Three practical changes can accomplish that but only if they are made at local district, school, and classroom levels. To be sure, state and federal education leaders can support local leaders by providing policy encouragement and resources, but only local school leaders and their faculties, in collaboration with their communities, can achieve the essential transformations. Here's how:

1. Historically, assessment has been seen only as a tool for judging the sufficiency of learning and for holding learners accountable. In the future, *teachers must also use assessment in their classrooms to help students learn.* This must become a priority.

2. It is time to abandon the belief that intimidation can work as a universal motivator; it has never worked well and never will. *Learning success is the only viable universal motivator* and we must help teachers understand effective ways to use this motivator in their classrooms.

3. The *quality of our assessments must improve* at all levels.

## LOCAL PRIORITY #1:
## USE "ASSESSMENT FOR LEARNING" TO PROMOTE ACADEMIC SUCCESS

Our traditional educational model held that teachers know and teach, as students listen and learn—or not. Teachers test to find out who mastered the material and who did not, record the results, dole out the rewards or punishments, and then move on to the next lesson. Essentially, adults control the classroom and students are receptacles. Those students who master the material early on can then build on that foundation to achieve further success. Students who miss the early learning continue to struggle as the instructional system marches on—leaving them farther and farther behind. According to this traditional model, assessment is something adults do to students because their assessment job is judge and grade the sufficiency of each student's learning.

In the 1990s, a small team of us working around the world began to ask, what if we made students more active players in monitoring their own learning success? What if we taught them the skills of self-evaluation so they could partner with their teachers in monitoring and regulating their own learning? What if assessment became something done *with* students, not merely to them? Would they then learn more?

What we have discovered is that self-evaluation is not only a strong confidence builder, motivator, and facilitator of learning, but it is also at the heart of academic competence in every school subject. Let me illustrate.

Below is a brief text passage taken from an exercise in Gillet and Tangle (1986). See if you can figure out what it's about.

For some it is highly unsettling to come into close contact with them. It is far worse to gain control over and deliberately inflict pain on them. The revulsion caused by this punishment is so strong that many will not take part in it at all. But there is one group of people who seem to revel in the contact and the punishment, as well as the rewards associated with both. Members of this group share modes of dress, talk and deportment. Then there is another group of people who shun the whole enterprise—contact, punishment and rewards alike. Members of this group are as varied as all humanity. But there also is a third group not previously mentioned for whose sake attention in this activity is undertaken. They too harm their victims, though they do so without intention of cruelty. They simply follow their own necessities. Theirs is the cruelest punishment of all. Sometimes, but not always, they themselves suffer as a result. (Gillet & Temple, 1986)

Almost everyone struggles with this reading task. The reason comprehension evades us in this case is that all of the proper nouns have been removed and only pronouns remain with no referents. This blocks comprehension. Here's why: In recent years, reading specialists have helped us understand the cognitive processes of reading comprehension more clearly. In order to comprehend a passage such as this, the reader must bring two things to the table: appropriate prior knowledge and a sufficiently well-developed text processing or decoding capability to mentally lift the author's meaning from the page.

With respect to prior knowledge, it can be said that we each carry in our brains personal mental copies of the world as we understand it, given our prior experiences and learning—our "schema" or "schemata."

As we read, we instantly and automatically (particularly as proficient readers) decode the words and sentences—the language—in order to draw the author's message from the page and we relate it to our schema in order to compare the two. When we read for learning, we continuously decide when and how to change our schema according to the lessons presented by our "teacher/author." When we read for pleasure, comprehension becomes a process of relying on our schema to visualize the story unfolding in our minds.

If the author has assumed that the reader possesses particular knowledge that the reader in fact does *not* possess, or if the text is written in an unfamiliar language, then no integration is possible, and there will be no comprehension. This is why, for many of us, reading a book on nuclear physics does not result in comprehension. We lack the proper knowledge base, including knowledge of vocabulary needed to make sense of the author's message.

Now let's return to that mysterious passage. Chances are, like most adult readers, you could process the sentences in a mechanical sort of way. There probably were no words or constructions that you had not seen before, yet despite that, the passage made no sense. Why? Without proper nouns, you had no links to the appropriate structure of prior knowledge (schema). In fact, you know what you need to know to figure out what the passage is about, and I am about to give you the link that will connect you to your schema. When I do, you will comprehend the meaning contained in every sentence.

But first, I want to make the essential point of this illustration. A few minutes ago when you were reading the passage, you probably began to realize pretty quickly that you were not understanding it, and when you realized that, you probably began to change reading strategies. Most common is re-reading. Some people just try to read more slowly. Still others try to plug in trial topics to see if that brings the meaning to the fore. In any case, *you kept monitoring your own comprehension to see if your new strategy was working any better* than the old one. The fact that you did so in the face of not comprehending represents compelling evidence that you have made yourself into an independently functioning adult reader. When confronted with a lack of understanding that *you detected on your own,* you went into problem solver mode to try to find a pathway to meaning.

What prompted your change of strategy? Your automatically triggered skill of self-assessment. You were monitoring your own comprehension and, when you determined you were not understanding the material, you began to change strategies. Assessment of one's own comprehension resides at the very heart of reading proficiency. Any student (indeed, any person) who cannot evaluate his or her own comprehension and respond strategically based on the results of that evaluation cannot become an independently functioning adult reader.

Each teacher's job is to turn over to her or his students the keys to the reading kingdom—to bring students to a place where they no longer need the teacher to give them a reading comprehension test to find out if they got it. We must bring students to a point where they can determine for themselves whether they are understanding and decide what to do about it when they are not.

Consider this same idea applied to the development of writing proficiency. A student who cannot monitor the quality of his or her own writing and revise it when it isn't "working" has not yet become an independently functioning writer. The teacher must help students master the keys to effective writing so they can apply these to their own work in a manner that frees them from the need for the teacher's judgment. The same holds true of math or science problem solving—or any other subject. Teachers must make sure their students reach a level of understanding that enables them to evaluate their own work and come up with remedies and solutions as needed, both for in the classroom and beyond.

Now I will tell you what that passage is about and I want you to go back and re-read it. As you do, you will be able to step back, monitor your own comprehension, and actually *watch yourself comprehending.* This passage is about the use of worms as bait for fishing. Now go back and re-read and then return here.

The crucial point here is that teachers have two key responsibilities: The first is to understand the critical elements that underpin academic success and to turn those keys to success over to their students in terms they can understand. The second is to help students develop proficiency in applying those critical elements to their own work so students can, over time, become independent performers—that is, lifelong learners.

How can teachers bring their students to this point of academic independence? By engaging students *as partners* in monitoring their own learning while it is unfolding. This way students can watch themselves grow, and feel—and be—in control of that growth.

## Assessment for Learning—Defined

To help students become effective monitors of their own learning, teachers can learn from the work of Australian professor Royce Sadler. He instructs us to teach in ways that make sure students always know the answers to the following questions *while they are learning:*

- Where am I going (that is, what am I trying to learn)?
- Where am I now on my journey to learning it?
- How can I close the gap between the two?

In recent decades, researchers and practitioners around the world have developed ways to help students monitor their own learning status by answering these questions. One of these practitioners is Jan Chappuis (2011), who articulates specific ways to make Professor Sadler's guidelines operational during learning in the classroom:

- Where am I going?
  1. Provide students with a clear understanding (student-friendly) of the learning target (e.g., a student-friendly rubric, guide, list of expectations, or set of objectives) from the very beginning of the learning.
  2. Provide examples or models of strong, mid-range, and weak student work in order to promote deeper understanding of the target.

- Where am I now?
  3. Offer students regular access to descriptive feedback focused on specific qualities of their work and inform them about how to do better the next time.
  4. Teach students to self-assess so they can monitor their own academic development, and to set goals so they can determine what comes next in their learning.

- How can I close the gap?
  5. Design lessons focused on one learning target at a time.
  6. Teach students to evaluate key features of their work.
  7. Teach students to observe and record changes in the quality of their work and provide opportunities to share that documentation with others.

In order to maximize the learning success of each student by using these strategies, teachers must believe without question that—

- (a) Students can hit any target that they can envision and that holds still for them;

- (b) Students who watch themselves progressing up the scale of success are more likely to keep trying because success keeps self-doubt at bay; and

(c) Students can manage and communicate about their own learning in ways that build confidence, engagement, and achievement.

When teachers empower students to track and control their own learning, both key instructional decision makers of the classroom come together to form a learning team. Because the assessment responsibility is shared, some of that work shifts to students, thus granting teachers more instructional time. Most importantly, students' sense of academic self-efficacy and achievement increases, boosting teachers' sense of professional achievement as well.

This discussion of Local Priority #1 has centered on the formative side of classroom assessment—how to use assessment to promote student success. Teachers also have responsibility for periodically judging whether students have met expectations so teachers can report that progress to parents—through report cards or other tools of summative assessment. Both summative and formative applications are significant, but they are different, and every classroom teacher needs to balance the two. That balance has not been our legacy but it can and must be our future.

# LOCAL PRIORITY #2: MOTIVATE WITH LEARNING SUCCESS, NOT INTIMIDATION

In American education, we often assume that students are not supposed to like school and, therefore, will not put forth effort to learn unless compelled to do so. Students are motivated with the promise of high report card grades if they learn and threatened with public embarrassment, as well as dire social and economic consequences, if they don't.

As a result, schools sometimes become places of entrapment and humiliation and teachers become people who manipulate students in order to control their learning behavior. In response, most students realize early that the way to minimize risk and vulnerability is to study and learn. If the risk of failure appears too great, or the embarrassment of being labeled a loser becomes too hurtful, the only way to avoid dire personal consequences is to get away. We have only to examine our dropout rates to see how many students have seen getting away as their only viable option.

This manipulation of personal vulnerability is clearly not a healthy, effective way to promote maximum learning for all, encouraging low achievers to rise up to narrow the achievement gap. We know how to maximize learning for our students, and it certainly is not by threatening or embarrassing them, especially struggling learners who are on losing streaks and don't believe they can succeed. Standing at the political podium screaming in a stentorian voice for higher test scores is not the answer. Holding teachers' salaries and even employment status hostage to scores on annual tests that may not even reflect the learning targets the teacher is responsible for teaching—tests that are almost certainly not sensitive enough to measure the influence of an individual teacher—is clearly not the answer.

What is the single biggest factor in determining the motivational impact of test results? The impact of assessment on learning turns on how students respond to assessment results. That emotional reaction will be productive if—and only if—a teacher has taken students to a place where they can say to themselves, "I understand these results and know what they tell me about my growth as a learner—and also what I need to learn next. What's more, I can handle this, and I'm going to keep trying." Students who can say these things to themselves after being assessed stand a strong chance of ultimately being successful.

What if, in place of that positive response, some students say this? "I don't know what this means, and I have no idea what to do next. I'm obviously too stupid to learn this anyway, and I quit." Hopelessness rules and once again, intimidation has failed to create any motivation whatsoever. Both student and teacher now have a serious problem, as the assessment results that were supposed to drive learning have just stopped it dead in its tracks.

Assessment is not only something adults do to students, it is something students do to themselves, too. Therefore, what students think about and do with assessment results is at least as important as what the adults think about and do with those results. They see the results and they make decisions, and it is up to teachers and other educators to ensure that those decisions are as positive and productive as possible. The key is creating a system of assessment for learning, which includes making students partners in the assessment process.

## Assessment for Learning—Applied

The purpose of student-involved assessment is that it can motivate productive action on the part of learners. This takes us back to Chappuis' (2009)[1] seven strategies for using assessment to promote learning.

*Strategy 1: Provide students with a clear*
*learning target from the outset.*

By providing students with an understanding of the learning target, we give them the first piece of information they need to measure the distance between where they are now and where they want to be. Just knowing where they are headed can be a confidence builder because learners feel more in control when they do not have to guess about their progress.

*Strategy 2: Provide examples of strong,*
*mid-range, and weak student work.*

By supplementing that description of the learning target with samples of student work depicting a range of quality from beginner (just barely made a start) to proficient (excellent work), we begin to build students' sense of the journey they are about to make. This makes their learning challenge ever clearer and more manageable. Further, picture samples of student work arrayed along an achievement continuum. With these in hand, students can break the journey down into a series of steps (none of them too big), and that increases students' own internal confidence.

*Strategy 3: Offer students regular descriptive*
*feedback as they learn.*

As learning continues, students need frequent helpful feedback. Notice that this is different from a judgment or grade. Good feedback gives students a clear picture of how their performance looks, how others see it, what specific characteristics or qualities stand out, get in the way, or make the performance work well. Such feedback helps students understand how to improve the quality of their work. It is also a vital steppingstone toward self-evaluation.

It is important that feedback occur during instruction. While learning is ongoing, teachers need to minimize judgmental feedback. During this assessment *for* learning process, the grade book is closed. It will be opened only when it's time to evaluate if the learning has been accomplished.

*Strategy 4: Teach students to self-assess.*

The crucial motivational step comes next: Given that students understand the target, have a sense of the steps they must take to reach it, and have the vocabulary needed to communicate about their progress, they are in a position to begin detecting both strengths (to build on) and deficiencies (to remedy) in their own work. In effect, they can begin to generate their own feedback and to become partners with the teacher in deciding what comes next in their learning. The sense of strong positive academic self-efficacy (control over one's own chances of academic success) that can arise from this step is especially powerful for struggling learners. The likely impact of effective (and often positive) self-assessment on a student, the desire to invest and succeed (read: positive motivation) takes a giant leap forward—and may never retreat again.

*Strategy 5: Design lessons focused on one*
*learning target at a time.*

As students assume some control of their learning, teachers become coaches, building lessons that help students advance the quality of their work one key skill at a time. This is what coaches do in practice: provide descriptive feedback and guided practice on individual skills—such as batting or catching—that later form a larger whole: baseball. The challenge for the teacher lies in identifying the specific individual skills that are important to a larger performance domain such as writing—and then finding ways to help students become more proficient at things such as choosing a topic, writing a lead, improving sentence flow, or editing faulty copy. Over time, the student acquires an ever larger repertoire of individual skills (dozens, if not hundreds of them), always connecting each to that bigger picture of writing (or reading, math, or whatever).

*Strategy 6: Teach students to evaluate*
*key features of their own work.*

The students' (a) understanding of the learning target, (b) continuous access to detailed feedback, and (c) sense of internal control over their advancement sets them up to manage improvement of their own work. The ability to assess one's own work and then reshape it to meet specified criteria contributes greatly to confidence.

*Strategy 7: Engage students in continuous self-reflection, tracking changes in the quality of their work.*

By providing students opportunities to track their growth and share what they discover with others, we enable them to bring all strategies to bear at once: their knowledge of the target and its critical elements, their sense of how the quality of work can evolve and how their work reflects that evolution, their understanding and use of the vocabulary needed to communicate about their own success, and, finally, their excitement at having successfully navigated the journey from beginner to proficient learner.

This scenario differs fundamentally from the one many adults experienced during school years, where often students were left to "psych out" the teacher or guess at what counted and therefore what to concentrate our studies on; where, if we guessed wrong we failed; where, very often, the final assessment bore little relationship to the content or priorities presented during instruction; where we remained uncertain about the grade we would receive until it arrived; where those who struggled received lots of Fs on their report cards, F's that were supposed to motivate them to try harder; where struggling students were on their own and mostly doomed to finish last—if they finished at all. We know better than this. We know how to help *all* students succeed, not just those at the top of the rank order.

## Once Again, Understand the Emotional Dynamics

It is important that we keep clearly in mind how this plays out in the mind of the learner. When principles of assessment for learning as outlined above are done well, they provide the learner with insights which trigger emotions that support learning. When they are missing or are done poorly, they fuel inferences on the part of the learner which trigger counter-productive emotions that stop learning.

When the learning "destination" and the pathway to success are clear it reduces anxiety because the learner is constantly able to track progress and knows that the target is within reach with continued effort. As the gap continues to reduce in the mind of the learner, it minimizes vulnerability—reduces the risk of failure. In other words, the student's consistent access to feedback shows the student how to continue to improve.

Students' involvement in the self-assessment process as they are learning supplies immediate and ongoing affirmation that their efforts are paying off—the sense of being on a winning streak. Students' sense of the productivity of their studies gives them a clear idea of when they need help and specifically what help they need.

Extended over the long term, other important benefits emerge. As students watch themselves grow, or not, succeed, or not, struggle, or not, they can evaluate their own interest in the learning target in question. In other words, they can evaluate their own ability or desire to master the domains they are studying. This can feed into thoughtful long-term educational planning. It can fuel ongoing optimism or initiate important changes in direction when needed.

On the other hand, when classroom assessment for learning features are missing or are done poorly, the result will be that learning stops. When students are left to guess at the learning destination, it leads to confused and unfocused actions on their part. If they don't know where they are going, the result can be frustration and learning stops. When the gap between where they are now and where the teacher wants them to be is too great in the mind of the students, they sense the risk and looming danger. This can trigger the inference that they cannot win and they will stop all efforts in that direction. When feedback is inadequate, performance does not improve, thus robbing learners of a sense of control over their own academic well-being. They don't know how to ask for help, and the result will be losing streaks, pessimism, and a sense of powerlessness. This is what dropping out is all about.

## LOCAL PRIORITY #3: MAXIMIZE CLASSROOM ASSESSMENT QUALITY

In my workshops over the years, as teachers begin to learn about issues of assessment quality, they report that I'm scaring them.

Asked why, they say the training is revealing to them that they have not been doing a good job of assessing the achievement of their students. In thirty years of this work, I have yet to meet a teacher who doesn't want to learn how to do it better. The problem is not motivation—it is lack of opportunity to learn.

Many things can go wrong in designing, developing, scoring, and using the results of any assessment. Each of these things can be done well or poorly, and there is nothing complicated about this. We know how to do these things well every time, and we know how to train teachers to do so. Following are descriptions of the four potential problems that teachers need to avoid in constructing assessments.

## Potential Quality Problem #1: The learning targets to be assessed are ill-defined.

Fuzzy or inappropriate targets make it impossible to build properly focused test items and scoring guides. Obviously, the test developer must fully understand the learning targets in order to develop good exercises and scoring schemes.

There are two troubling learning target problems that need to be considered because they have a direct impact on school quality and testing practices. One centers on the number of targets and the other on how they are defined at testing time.

*Too many targets given available resources*

Put a team of content specialists in one room and ask them to define what it is important for students to learn in their discipline and at their grade level, and the result will be a list of achievement standards that students realistically cannot be expected to master, given the time and other resources available. This has given rise to assessment problems in American education for decades, especially in the content domains that make up the lifelong learner proficiencies about which we care so much: reading, writing, and math problem solving. Here is what typically happens, as recounted by one middle school teacher from California.

As an educator, I feel immense pressure to cover as much as I can before state testing in April. Most educators I know have an overall map/timeline of what should be covered before state testing. I know that once the state testing is close, I am guilty of cramming as much as possible into the few days before in hopes that they will at least remember some of it. Why does it cover an entire year of material but then they test us before that year is over? I teach 7th grade math—a huge range of concepts to cover in 180 school days. There is hardly enough time to cover them, let alone give the students time to master them. (S. Gandolfo, personal communication, 2013)

The negative impact of this state of affairs is not limited to annual state testing. It will impact the quality and effectiveness of teachers' use of day-to-day classroom assessments as well. When this happens, local school districts have only one viable course of action. Set local priorities; that is, select the highest priority achievement standards, make sure those are covered first and best, and then get to the rest as resources permit.

What if the targets selected for coverage on the state's accountability test do not match those developed by the school district? There is only one viable course of action: go to the state and tell them that their test is not a valid indicator of the achievement of students in this school district and ask them what they intend to do to fix it. All of the alternatives to this approach place students at risk, due to the potential mismeasurement of their achievement.

### Learning target definitions are too broad

The second learning target problem deals with testing traditions that define achievement expectations as mastery of broad content domains. Standardized tests have tended to yield gross scores in domains labeled, "Reading," "Mathematics," "Science," and so on. Within each domain, there are many priority achievement standards that make up the learning targets of that content area. Test developers write items to sample as many of those standards as the very few minutes of available testing time will permit. This means some standards will not be tested at all and those that are will be covered only by an item or two. But nevertheless, the developers assemble those items into that particular test's representation or definition of the total domain.

Put another way, because of practical time constraints, there is never sufficient time to include test items covering all standards that may fall within broad domains, nor can tests typically include enough items covering any one standard to permit us to make confident judgments about student mastery of that standard.

For this reason, at the accountability level of testing and indeed at every level of assessment development and use, if we wish to support student learning, the assessor's goal should be to gather enough samples of student work to inform users about *how each student did in mastering each relevant learning target*. That means the test needs to include enough exercises per standard to lead the teacher to a confident inference about each student's level of mastery. With relatively simple, straightforward targets, that may be just one exercise, or it may require a dozen or more. It depends on the standard. But if a test is to be instructionally helpful, then it needs to suggest to the teacher what comes next in each student's learning.

## Potential Quality Problem #2: Using the wrong assessment method given the learning target(s).

Available assessment methods include multiple choice items, essay exercises, performance observations, and direct personal interaction, and some work well with certain kinds of learning but not with others. If the developer is not schooled on what method to use when, quality suffers.

As discussed, in the United States we have relied heavily on multiple choice tests, and this predilection is understandable. Such tests are relatively fast to develop and inexpensive to score. When a hundred thousand students are to take a state assessment, cost is an issue, to be sure. It is crucial to understand, however, that when one begins test development with a decision that multiple choice will be the method used, it restricts the range of learning targets that can be tested to content knowledge and a few simple patterns of reasoning. Relatively more complex standards such as those centered on complex reasoning proficiency and performance skills simply cannot be measured in a multiple choice format.

What if curriculum achievement standards include these kinds of learning, as they most always do—and certainly should.

These require essay tests, performance assessments, and assessments that rely on direct verbal interaction. The demands of college and workplace training our children face as we look to the future require that they develop such complex reasoning abilities. Their teachers must be ready to assess their mastery of those kinds of learning targets as their students develop them.

Just to clarify, there is nothing inherently wrong with multiple choice testing per se. Multiple choice tests (like any other forms of tests) are fine in the hands of competent users and in the appropriate context; that is, when the target is appropriate and when there is a clear right or best answer to a direct question. But they are a formula for disaster in the wrong context or in the hands of a naïve user.

## Potential Quality Problem #3:
## Poor quality test items and/or scoring schemes.

If it is to be a multiple choice test, it needs to include only high quality items. If it is to be an essay test, we need good questions and scoring guidelines. So it is with each available assessment method. Pre-service teacher and administrator training programs absolutely must include training in the development of assessments, but in the absence of prior preparation, local in-service programs must become a priority. Professional development is available from many publishers and vendors, such as the Pearson Assessment Training Institute, Solution Tree, and Battelle for Kids (battelleforkids.org), and Corwin, among others.

Neither teacher nor administrator licensing examinations typically certify competence in assessment, so we have a national faculty and staff largely unschooled in the accurate assessment of student learning and in the use of the assessment process to both support and verify student learning. This must change.

## Potential Quality Problem #4:
## Ineffective communication of assessment results.

When test results are to feed into instructional decisions specifically intended to support student learning (as with assessment for learning), communication of those results must convey precise detail. In this context, results that take the form of total scores will not deliver the information needed.

Problems also arise if the communication of results is delayed for a long time. Students don't stop growing after they take the annual state test, so those test results that arrive weeks or even months after the test is administered no longer reflect students' achievement status. While teachers often fully intend to use results to modify their instruction, they cannot do so when the results don't arrive until the school year is nearly at an end. Timely feedback is important.

Further, we can anticipate problems when test scores are communicated to a user (decision maker) who doesn't understand what those scores mean—and who therefore cannot interpret them properly.

Clearly, those who have not mastered sound communication of assessment results place students directly in harm's way. Most teachers and many administrators have not been given the opportunity to learn about this either.

In summary, then, quality assessments are created by those who begin with clear and appropriate learning targets, select proper assessment methods, build quality assessments, and communicate results effectively given their intended purpose.

### Our History of Ineffective Remedies

For decades, the education community has tried to make up for the lack of assessment literacy by, for example, including ready-made assessments in published text materials or by providing teachers with libraries or banks of test items they can use to build the tests they need. Unfortunately, these assessments are (a) often developed by those who also lack assessment literacy and so lack quality control standards, and (b) do not align with students' and teachers' daily informational needs in time to influence instruction. Here's the bottom line: *Unless teachers can create quality assessments on their own and consistently weave them effectively into ongoing teaching and learning, student achievement will suffer.*

## WHO CAN/MUST LEAD
## THE CHANGE PROCESS?

Several local players hold the keys to completing the three changes identified in this chapter: local community leaders; policy makers at local, state, and federal levels; school leaders; teachers; and those in higher education who train professional educators.

*Local communities* (parents, grandparents, taxpayers) can take the lead by asking their local school board, administrators, and teachers the following questions:

About Local Priority #1 focused on *why we assess:*

- Do our schools have a policy requiring a balance of formative assessment (to support learning) and summative assessment (to certify it) in our classrooms? If not, what is our plan for instituting such a policy?
- Are our school leaders trained and qualified to achieve this balance? If not, what are our professional development plans?
- Can and do our teachers use classroom assessments both to support and to certify student learning? Again, if not and given that our teachers need this expertise, what is our professional development plan?

About Local Priority #2, *motivating with learning success:*

- Are our teachers trained to engage students in using high quality assessment to support their own learning—and eventually certify their own competence? If not, when and how will they be trained?
- How do we motivate all of our students for productive learning?
- What, specifically, are we doing to motivate struggling learners?

About Local Priority #3, *quality assessments:*

- What is the quality of day-to-day classroom assessments?
- Are our school leaders qualified to evaluate those assessments? If so, are we doing a good job of assessing throughout our schools and classrooms? If not, what is our plan for doing a better job?
- Are our teachers and principals schooled in the principles of sound assessment practice?
- Do our hiring criteria include assessment competence?

If answers generated locally are unsatisfying after reading this book, consider assertive action through school site councils, consultation with district leadership, and meetings with school board members. Consider a task force to delve into local assessment practices or to review the district's school improvement plan and evaluate what it says about assessment quality and use.

As this local activity is being conducted *federal, state, and local policy makers* might profitably seek out information about what teachers need to know and be able to do to use assessment in new ways to support student learning. Consider reexamination of teacher and administrator training standards and requirements, as well as the criteria used in the certification and hiring of these practitioners.

*Local school district administrators* can take the lead, first, by evaluating your own professional level of assessment literacy and acting on the results as needed. Then make sure conditions are in place within your district to make assessment a productive part of teaching and learning. Are your learning targets clear and appropriate? Is your policy environment driving sound practice? Are your teachers assessment literate, and are they ready to communicate assessment results (to students, parents, school boards, administrators, and one another) in ways that support and certify achievement, depending on the context?

*Teachers* can take the lead by evaluating and maximizing your own assessment literacy. If you find it necessary, go to your supervisor and seek concrete and specific opportunities to learn. One of the most important outcomes of professional development in this realm can be time savings through (a) greater classroom assessment efficiency, and (b) students' responsibility for their own assessment (in partnership with you) while they are learning.

## THIS IS PERSONAL

One gloomy winter afternoon, our daughter, Krissy, arrived home from third grade full of gloom herself. She said she knew we were going to be angry with her. Then she held out a sheet of paper—the third-grade size with the wide lines. On it, she had written a story.

Upon inquiring, we found out that her assignment was to write about someone or something she cared about deeply. She wrote of Kelly, an adorable kitten who had come to be part of our family, but who had to return to the farm after two weeks because of allergies.

On the sheet of paper was an emergent writer's version of this story—not sophisticated, but poignant. Krissy's recounting of events was accurate and her story conveyed her sadness and disappointment at losing her new little friend.

At the bottom of the page, which filled about three quarters of the page, was a big red circled "F." We asked her why she had gotten that grade and she told us that the teacher said she was to fill the page with writing and she only used two-thirds. Her teacher had added that Krissy had better learn to follow directions or she would continue to fail.

When she had finished telling Nancy and me this story, Krissy put the sheet of paper down on the kitchen table and, with a discouraged look, said in a totally intimidated voice, "I'll never be a good writer anyway," and left the room.

Though her grade certainly did not reflect it, Krissy had succeeded at hitting an important target, at least at some level, because she produced some pretty good writing. But her confidence in herself as a writer was deeply shaken because her teacher confused one expectation that students comply with directions with a second, and unrelated, expectation that they learn to write well. Let's analyze this event in a bit more detail.

In this case, the primary focus of the assessment was on controlling student behavior, not advancing academic achievement. (Had that not been the case, the teacher would surely have commented on the writing.) Krissy didn't know that following directions precisely took precedence over writing well. Further, the learning target to be assessed was length, not quality. Krissy didn't understand that either. The governing evaluation criterion was "Fill the page," not "Write well." As a result, both the assessment and the feedback had a negative impact on this young student. Without question, it is quite easy to see if a page is full, but was that (or should that be) the point? Should we assess what is easy to measure or what is important? It is challenging to assess something as complicated as writing and to formulate and deliver understandable and timely feedback that helps a student not only improve, but also remain confident about her ability to grow as a writer.

In sum, the purpose was not clear, the learning target was not clear, the assessment was of inferior quality due to unclear performance criteria, and, as a result, the feedback delivered to the learner was destructive. It took a long time for us to work our way through this and to help Kris believe there was a pretty good writer trapped in there. Fast forward to high school English class and Kris's first term paper assignment.

In this situation, Kris's assignment was to read three literary pieces by the same author, develop a thesis statement, and defend it with evidence from the literary works. Note the role that assessment played as a teacher in this case.

The teacher began by distributing copies of a term paper that was of outstanding quality. The students' homework assignment that evening was to read it and try to discern what made it outstanding. The next day in class the students brainstormed, coming up with a long list of characteristics. The next homework assignment was to boil that list down—to group the characteristics into the five or six categories that really governed quality. The next day in class they argued about that final short list, finally arriving at consensus. They included qualities such as the paper's organization and use of supportive evidence, among others.

Next came the teamwork. Students were grouped into teams of five or six, and each team was assigned one of the categories. Their job was to define that criterion and describe as concisely as possible what a term paper would look like if it (a) was outstanding with respect to their characteristic, (b) was of poor quality, or (c) was in the middle. Teams took turns sharing their work with the class and refining it as they went. The keys to success were becoming clearer to the students as they developed definitions and rating scales. Notice that these were developed by students, not simply handed to them by the teacher.

On the following day, the teacher shared copies of a term paper she had fabricated that was of dismal quality. Homework assignment: Read and evaluate the paper using the agreed upon criteria. What kept that paper from working? What needed revision? Students shared their analyses the next day in class.

Finally, the teacher instructed them to begin drafting their papers, keeping the evaluation criteria they had developed together clearly in mind. As they drafted, they worked in pairs and small teams to review each other's papers, providing feedback, again, in terms of the specific criteria that characterized a quality paper. The teacher also offered to review anyone's draft and provide feedback on any one of the criteria if requested to do so.

Focused revision continued in this manner until students were ready to submit their papers. A submission deadline was suggested, but it could be extended through negotiation with the teacher. Her perspective was this: If you treat young people like adults, they will behave like adults. This is an assessment literate teacher.

Can you anticipate the quality of the papers these students produced? They were almost all outstanding.

The differences between what happened here and what happened with Kris's third grade kitten story obviously are substantial. In high school, in contrast to third grade, the learning target was clear and the teacher made sure it was understood by the learners. That understanding was deepened through student involvement in defining the criteria that would indicate strong performance and through their study of samples of work. Focused revision was interspersed with descriptive feedback, improving the quality of each paper during the writing process. The results were more than a set of term papers that received high grades, as the experience spawned a group of more confident writers. This kind of growth and self-awareness (not to mention the ability to coach others) can happen for every student in every classroom.

An elementary school teacher from Washington state described the impact of these practices on the achievement of his students in a similar manner:

Within the first month that I began using formative assessment practices in my classroom I saw achievement gains from virtually all students, with the greatest gains being made by the lowest achieving students. Using these practices has completely changed the learning environment in my classroom. Good instruction is still important, but the focus has shifted from teaching to learning and from the teacher to the student. Now that learning targets are clear to students they are able to take responsibility for meeting those targets. By regularly reflecting on where they are in relation to the targets they are able to decide what action they need to take or what help they need in moving forward to meet those targets.

Formative assessment has removed barriers to learning in my classroom . . . [my] students now know that, when they take responsibility for their own learning, they can be successful. (B. Herzog, personal communication, 2013)

## Assessment for Twenty-First Century Schools

This analysis issues a very serious indictment of assessment in American education, calling out and demanding assertive action from those who can turn our assessment systems around: policy makers and professional educators at federal, state, and local levels, parents and community leaders, the academic community, and the academic and commercial testing community. If I have angered you, I urge you to analyze why. Whose interests should we be thinking of and protecting in our assessment practices?

We have established the evaluation criteria for judging the quality of local school district assessment systems. Now local leaders must gather the local evidence, and make your judgments about what needs to change in your system. We know how to build balanced local assessment systems that both promote and certify student learning—that is, that link assessment to teaching, learning, and student well-being. Good practice involves much more than valid and reliable once-a-year test scores. There is no question, we know better and can do better.

## ENDNOTE

1. From Chappuis, J., *Seven Strategies of Assessment for Learning*, 1st edition, © 2009. Adapted by permission of Pearson Education, Inc., Upper Saddle River, NJ.

# 7

# A Concluding Message to the Measurement Community

*Leaders must encourage their organizations to dance to music not yet heard.*

Warren G. Bennis

**An introductory note:** Even though you may not be a member of this professional community, I hope you will read on. If you agree with my recommendations, promote discussions of them in your own educational forums. . . .

We in the measurement community stand at a fork in the road: Will we be leaders in the development of increasingly effective schools or merely the shepherds of "data" used by others charged with improving schools? Our collective history has cast us in the role of data tenders. Our job has been to maximize the quality of test results. But if we wish, we can do so much more to improve the quality of assessments throughout the educational system, and we can add our assessment processes to the school improvement equation as instructional interventions.

With respect to matters of assessment quality, as rigorous as our standards of validity and reliability have become, they play no role in the development or use of assessments in a vast majority of testing contexts in American education. For example, we remain almost totally ineffective in convincing teacher preparation faculties and faculties of educational administration that assessment literacy is an essential part of the foundation of effective instruction and therefore should be part of their pre-service preparation programs. As a result, our standards of test quality have rarely found their way into the classrooms of American schools—and this is not only a problem in K–12 education. Institutional norm or expectation for quality classroom assessment are rare in higher education, even in colleges of education. Why have our standards of good practice not penetrated teaching and learning in these centers of higher education?

We have watched as politicians and policy makers set assessment policy at local, state, and federal levels that is virtually indefensible. The current, popular demand in teacher evaluation that annual standardized test scores serve as the index of teacher impact on student achievement is a classic example. As keepers of the quality assessment flame, are we really powerless to assert our standards of quality in the halls of political power?

We have sold tests and associated services to state and local educators whom we know are not trained or qualified to use them productively. Is our role merely to satisfy their need to comply with state or federal accountability demands or is it to assure quality assessment is effectively used to benefit students? Can we not demand assessment literacy of our clients and help them develop it?

We have spent years writing, refining, and then publishing standards of excellence in testing that apply only to a small fraction of the assessments that happen in a student's academic life—the high-stakes standardized tests—while we ignore the other 99 percent of them: those tests developed and used in classrooms day to day to drive instruction. Surely translations of the standards into common sense ideas described in everyday language are in order.

We point to technology as an important key to the production and use of quality assessments, and, to be sure, ideas such as computer adaptive applications are exciting and are being helpful. But these tools of the digital realm will only be helpful if applied in the context where the assessors have developed a clear understanding of the learning targets involved. A counter example: The English Language Arts community is up in arms about the idea of computer scoring of student writing samples—and for good reason. Such a scoring practice reflects a fundamental lack of sense regarding the target. Writing is not merely about the mechanics of expression—it is also very much about making ideas clear, using language beautifully, crafting focused sentences, and moving readers. Human judgment, not computer software, is required for sound evaluation of something so complex and nuanced.

In effect, we have permitted, even encouraged, the perception that measurement's prime role is in revealing the effects of teaching while overlooking the emerging reality that it also can be a means through which students learn. The two are not the same. The former reflects achievement status while the latter seeks to change achievement status.

We must continue to tear down the barriers between the measurement community and the teaching profession. Teachers and school leaders drive school quality; the measurement community does not. We can only make our contribution to school improvement through them, and we can help them by transforming complex technical validity and reliability concepts into common sense terms that practitioners can master, embrace, and use in their own classrooms. More specifically, we can develop our capacity to be of direct service to them by expanding or refining our thinking and theirs in the following ways:

**1. Think more broadly about why we assess. See the assessment process as a means through which students learn, not merely as a measure of the effect of teaching.** We have thought and have encouraged others to think of assessment as something that comes at the end of teaching in order to evaluate its impact. Our community's jargon reveals this tendency: end of unit tests, end of semester projects, end of course exams, annual springtime state accountability tests, college admissions exams towards the end of high school.

This focus on assessment as a terminal event has had the effect of limiting our impact on school quality. It has stifled our thinking about why we assess and for whom, how we carry it out, and how we share and use results.

The alternative is to think of assessment as an instructional intervention. The dominant version of this idea has been to see formative assessment as more frequent and focused periodic testing to help teachers refine instruction. Such applications certainly can be useful but also are limiting.

If we expand our vision of formative assessment to include student/teacher partnerships, we can empower students to understand the learning targets, gather continuous evidence of their growth, recognize how to move consistently forward toward success, make instructional decisions that enhance their own learning, and feel—at long last—in control of their own academic well-being. Student self-assessment is an important learning experience; it promotes success instead of merely measuring it. The act of self-assessment can change the performance being measured in very positive directions.

The vast majority of practicing teachers and school leaders are not familiar with such applications of assessment, and I urge that we in the measurement community (a) expand our collective vision of excellence in assessment to include these kinds of classroom applications, and (b) help practitioners learn to use them wisely and well.

**2. Assure that our standards of assessment quality are understood and applied in all assessment contexts.** Matters of assessment quality and test score dependability define the field of educational measurement. Over the decades, we have developed an array of sophisticated standards of reliability and validity; however, as suggested above, we have limited the quality control focus to only a fraction of the assessments that happen in a student's academic life: the very high-stakes, high visibility, and politically-driven local, state, national, and international accountability standardized achievement tests. This is understandable given the influence that results of such tests appear to wield and given that this has been the only context in which resources have been available for psychometricians to develop, try out, and refine their technical models. But, in effect, this has caused the field to shift almost entirely to large-scale standardized testing applications.

Historically, classroom assessments have been all but ignored in our published *Test Standards* and in our advocacy on behalf of good assessment practice. By and large, those assessments have been carried out in an almost complete quality control vacuum, as few practitioners have been given the opportunity to learn about gathering dependable evidence or using the assessment process or its results to support learning. As a result, it is safe to assume that achievement has been mismeasured and student learning has been compromised. After nearly a century of development and refinement, our quality control standards still have not made it into classrooms where almost all educational assessment takes place. This must change.

**3. Verify the instructional efficacy of assessment by demonstrating its effect on learning . . . in *each* context of application.** When school improvement researchers develop new instructional ideas, they are expected to carry out the rigorous scientific research needed to demonstrate that their intervention actually results in higher student achievement.

We addressed this earlier. Such research has not been reported for the school improvement intervention called "annual standardized testing," but so strong has been society's blind faith in the benefits of such tests that over the decades that I can find no one who has demanded or proposed it, let alone conducted it. The next generation of specialists must conduct that research, demonstrating the instructional efficacy of this vision of excellence in assessment by estimating its effect on student achievement.

To conduct this kind of research, investigators would have to invest whatever it takes to create, implement, score, and analyze a far more in-depth, comprehensive program of assessment of achievement than has been available in the past. It would need to center on important outcomes and rely on the full array of assessment methods. This can be done on a manageable scale in limited and carefully cost-controlled research settings—experimental and control. Without this background evidence of efficacy, annual tests cannot be fairly labeled school improvement tools.

This same research question remains relevant for classroom assessment. In this case, significant impact research already has been conducted and the effect sizes are promising, but some of these findings are being questioned and further investigation of effects is in order. In fact, there are few places where a sufficient foundation of local classroom assessment literacy has been put in place to permit a solid scientific test of the efficacy of this classroom intervention. For this reason, professional development in sound classroom assessment practice must remain a high priority at the local level. Only then will we be able to continue to test the proposition that classroom assessment can be a productive teaching tool.

**4. Design assessments in ways that permit inferences about student mastery of specific learning targets rather than domains of content or broad collections of standards.** Our traditional practice has been to sample broad achievement domains with assessment exercises reflective of enough targets to permit generalization about student mastery of all of the targets that make up that domain. When this evidence is sufficient to inform the educational decisions hanging in the balance in a particular testing context, such as annual accountability testing, then this sampling strategy adds efficiency to the testing process and, therefore, makes sense.

The question is, for how many of the instructional decisions that contribute to student learning success is this form of sampling appropriate? When we think about the array of assessment users whose decisions truly impact students, the answer is very few.

The kinds of results that help teachers support student learning inform about specific learning targets or standards their students have and have not mastered. Such results are narrowly focused and descriptive, not judgmental. They fit well into a context where students are ascending learning progressions and where they and their teachers need to know at any point in time where each student is now in relation to where we want them to be. Truly useful results inform them about what comes next in the learning. Both students and teachers must understand and be able to act upon the inferences such feedback permits, and this calls for assessments that sample focused learning targets rather than broad domains of them. In this sense, it is time for us to rethink our vision of the learning targets we should be sampling.

**5. Expand the criteria used to judge the quality of an assessment beyond characteristics of the score and the inferences scores permit to consideration of the impact of the results on students and their learning.** We evaluate the quality of assessments, in large part, based on the stability of the evidence they yield and the strength of the inferences they permit us to draw about student achievement. We seek valid inferences based on reliable evidence. In this respect, our quality-control concern is focused on the results of assessments, and if the results are of high quality (in this respect), we consider our measurement job to be done. We send the results to the users and move on to the next testing project.

But what if the results are not understood, are misunderstood, or are misused due to circumstances we in the measurement community might have prevented? What if the cause is the assessment illiteracy of the users? More troubling, what if our most valid and reliable test causes a student—or many students—to give up in hopelessness and to stop trying because of the way they are used locally? How can we consider this a quality assessment when it does more of this kind of harm than good?

The extent to which any test is suited to and appropriate for its intended context is a critical variable in determining the quality of any assessment. Context includes a match between assessment and its purpose together with the qualifications of the user to administer and interpret results of that assessment effectively. This suggests that a test's quality cannot be evaluated independent of the situation in which it is used. If that match is weak, then regardless of the technical adequacy of the test being used, it cannot be considered a quality assessment.

If we in the measurement community know that such problems exist with a particular application of a test, do we not have a professional and moral responsibility to speak out? As providers of data, we must also monitor the quality of the application and impact of our assessments on student well-being. Where students are at risk because of the likelihood of inept use, we should not permit our tests to be used. I am proposing a gatekeeper function for test providers that takes the form of an evaluation of the capacity of the users to use the test effectively.

**6. We must move beyond seeing assessment merely as something adults do to students and understand that it is something students constantly do to themselves.** The measurement community, in league with the leaders of school improvement initiatives, has long believed and promoted the perspective that if we just get the right test scores into the hands of teachers and school leaders, they will make the instructional decisions that will make schools work effectively. This is fine as far as it goes, as local educators who are making key decisions and decisions based on good evidence of achievement are likely to improve learning. But this way of thinking leaves key players out of the decision making process.

Students constantly evaluate their own achievement, too. They attend to adults' assessments of them, and they make key instructional decisions about how—indeed, whether—to continue with their own learning based on their own self-assessment and interpretation of the available evidence. The outcome can be hope or hopelessness, optimism or pessimism, an expectation of success or failure, regarding one's chances of future learning success. Depending on that internal judgment, students will either gain or lose confidence, increase or decrease engagement and effort, and experience learning success or failure. Their sense of themselves in the immediate learning context drives their subsequent actions. I believe our mission as a measurement community should be to help practitioners learn to use our assessments to keep students believing that success is within reach if they keep striving.

## SUMMARY AND CONCLUSION

Collectively, we must come to understand that, when the objective is to use assessment to enhance student learning, assessments work best when—

- The assessment environment is seen by all involved as wanting to promote maximum student success
- Each assessment is designed to meet pre-determined informational needs of the intended user(s)
- They provide a dependable representation of student achievement
- The user understands the results and knows how to use them productively
- Results focus on mastery of relatively narrowly defined and valued curricular learning targets versus broad achievement domains
- They provide a continuous flow of useful feedback versus once-a-year or infrequent judgments of achievement

- Results arrive in an immediately useable form versus a form that requires extensive local interpretation and analysis
- Students are directly involved in assessment of their learning as they are growing

As those who follow us view assessment twenty years from now, will they see students completing more test prep courses to prepare for the big test or will they see students taking charge of their own learning, assessing themselves accurately, coaching classmates, leading their own parent/teacher conferences, and seeing their teachers as their coaches and mentors? We are at a crossroad, and I hope the choice of direction is obvious.

## EPILOGUE: JUST ONE MORE STORY

This story was told to me by a middle school teacher years ago and reflects her belief in and reliance on student-led parent/teacher conferences—an idea which represents one of the most powerful breakthroughs in communicating about student learning in a long time.

The teacher, we'll call her Faye, refined a carefully articulated array of achievement standards, including descriptions of those targets in student-friendly terms. She also developed a strong foundation in assessment literacy. Finally, she consistently applied principles of assessment for learning during instruction, helping students know where they were going, where they were now, and how to close the gap between the two.

As learning began and as soon as students understood each learning target, she engaged them in an ongoing self-assessment process, so the students could watch themselves grow and become partners in understanding what came next in their learning. As they progressed up the scale of competence, she had them store samples of their ever-changing work, along with self-reflections on changes in their own learning, in their growth portfolios.

These portfolios became the basis for parent/teacher conferences near the end of the year, but she did not share the evidence of growth, her students did. They prepared carefully to describe to their parents (a) the evidence of their improvement, and (b) their understanding of what would come next in their learning.

Students invited their parents to the meeting, prepared their materials for presentation, managed introductions, and led a step-by-step review of their work. Since time constraints precluded Faye from meeting with each family, she had several conferences underway at one time while she hovered and listened, offering details or corroboration when needed. Faye also offered parents a separate one-on-one meeting with her if they wished it.

Following is the simple but powerful story: One of her students arrived for his conference with his entire family in tow: Mom, Dad, Gramma (he called her), and younger brother and sister. They were an immigrant family, and to Faye's surprise, her student began the conference in the family's native language—a language Faye did not speak. As she watched and listened with fascination, everything seemed to flow smoothly. Her student described his work as it was improving, his family asked questions, and Gramma nodded approvingly—even little brother and sister remained tuned in.

At one point when they took a break, Faye was able to ask her student if there was a particular reason that he was using his native language, and he said it was because Gramma did not speak English and he wanted her to be proud of him.

At the end of the conference, Faye recounts, there was brief family applause. As they exited the room, Faye stood at the door thanking them for coming. Gramma was last in line, and she took Faye's hand with a tear in her eye, squeezed it, and said thank you in a most sincere way and in her native language.

This certainly is not the vision of excellence in assessment that has dominated our work over the past several decades in the measurement community or in our schools and classrooms. Our collective sense of the role played by educational measurement in American schools has certainly not been that assessment is itself an important tool for learning. But if we seek to provide equal educational opportunities in an increasingly diverse society and to develop lifelong learners, this is the vision of our assessment future we must embrace.

# References

Absolum, M., Flockton, L., Hattie, J., Hipkins, R., & Reid, I. (2009). *Directions for assessment in New Zealand: Developing students' assessment capabilities.* Wellington, NZ: New Zealand Ministry of Education.

Bandura, A. (1994). Self-efficacy. In V. S. Ramachaudran (ed.) *Encyclopedia of human behavior* (Vol. 4, pp. 71–81). New York: Academic Press.

Black, P., & Wiliam, D. (1998). Assessment and classroom learning. *Educational Assessment: Principles, Policy and Practice, 5*(1), 7–74. Also summarized in Black & Wiliam (1998), Inside the black box: Raising standards through classroom assessment. *Phi Delta Kappan, 80*(2), 139–148.

British Columbia Ministry of Education. (2013). *Students must be at the centre of their learning.* Vancouver, BC: Author.

Chappuis, J. (2009). *Seven strategies of assessment for learning.* Portland, OR: Pearson Assessment Training Institute.

Gillet, J. W., & Temple, C. A. (1986). *Understanding reading problems: Assessment and instruction.* Boston: Little, Brown.

Hattie, J., & Timperley, H. (2007). The power of feedback. *Review of Research in Education.* Retrieved October 9, 2007 from https://rer.sagepub.com/content/77/1/81.full.pdf+html

Kanter, R. M. (2004). *Confidence: How winning and losing streaks begin and end.* New York: Crown Business.

New York Principals. (2013). *An open letter to parents of children throughout New York State regarding grade 3–8 testing.* Retrieved from www.newyorkprincipals.org/letter-to-parents-about-testing

Stiggins, R. J., & Chappuis, J. (2012). *An introduction to student-involved assessment for learning.* Columbus, OH: Pearson Education.

U.S. Department of Education. (2011). *Trends in high school dropout and completion rates.* Washington, D.C: National Center for Educational Statistics.

# Index

# CORWIN
## A SAGE Company

The Corwin logo—a raven striding across an open book—represents the union of courage and learning. Corwin is committed to improving education for all learners by publishing books and other professional development resources for those serving the field of PreK–12 education. By providing practical, hands-on materials, Corwin continues to carry out the promise of its motto: **"Helping Educators Do Their Work Better."**